VUSI

VUSI THEMBEKWAYO

VUSI

BUSINESS & LIFE LESSONS
FROM A BLACK DRAGON

Tafelberg

Also by Vusi Thembekwayo
The Magna Carta of Exponentiality

Tafelberg, an imprint of NB Publishers,
a division of Media24 Boeke Pty (Ltd),
40 Heerengracht, Cape Town, South Africa
www.tafelberg.com

Copyright © Vusi Thembekwayo

All rights reserved.
No part of this book may be reproduced or transmitted in any form or
by any electronic or mechanical means, including photocopying and
recording, or by any other information storage or retrieval system,
without written permission from the publisher.

First edition, first impression 2018
Third impression 2018

ISBN: 978-0-624-0-7771-8
Epub: 978-0-624-0-7772-5
Mobi: 978-0-624-0-7773-2

My life has been a collage of random luck, accidents, consistent self-doubt, mistakes, opportunities, chance meetings, and the odd bout of fortitude and hard work.

To the Queen, I love you, Ma.

To the 'govers', daddy loves.

To the Thembekwayo clan, thank you for raising a warrior bo-Dlamane.

This book is dedicated to the poor child growing up in the lowly streets of the shanty town, without hope, without opportunity and without love.

You too matter.

You too are capable.

You can change the world.

VT

Contents

1	The Gift of Having Nothing to Lose	9
2	To Show Your Best at Your Worst	23
3	Shine, Vusi, Shine!	35
4	The Lie of the Land	49
5	To Lead is to Learn to Command the Silence	61
6	The Attitude Adjustment Klap	73
7	There is no B in 'Team'	89
8	A Kota Loaf is Better than None	105
9	The Emperor Needs New Clothes	121
10	A Letter to Africa	135
	About the Author	141

1

The Gift of Having Nothing to Lose

*Why the fastest slave wins the race;
lessons from the vampire economy; and
the truth about the shape of the world*

He charges down the track in a blaze of colour – green for the land, gold for the sun, black for the colour of who he is and what he is better than anyone else in the world at doing: a black man, running for his life.

His arms cut the air like blades, his legs pump up and down like the pistons of a steam locomotive. He is a machine, made from flesh and blood. He is as human as you and me, but when he crosses the line, he turns into a god. He stands with his feet planted firmly on the ground; he leans back; he angles his right arm, taut and strong, in an archer's grip, and he points to the heavens, from where he draws his fire.

His name is Bolt. Lightning Bolt. Usain Lightning Bolt. At the 2016 Olympics in Rio, he ran the 100 metres in 9,81 seconds, to become, once again, the fastest man on earth.

You and I, as human as we may be in our limitations, as godlike in our ambitions, will not easily wrest the title from him. Just as we are unable to out-lightning Bolt – and I speak for myself here, your abilities may vary – so are we unable to out-think Einstein, out-box Muhammad Ali, out-sing Beyoncé.

But all of us are capable of striving, and striving begins with asking the big, nagging questions that have bothered us from when we were young: how and why? How, in this case, did Bolt get to be so unstoppable, so unbeatable? And why, as it turns out, is he only one of a whole breed of super-sprinters to have emerged from the island nation of Jamaica?

To begin with, we learn from Bolt that excellence is a moving target, that you pursue it with grim discipline and daily rigour, in the knowledge that there will always be someone in your shadow waiting for you to stumble and fall. We learn that he became a winner, and the only athlete in history to strike gold in the 100 metres in three consecutive Olympics, because he couldn't picture himself not winning. 'I don't want to come in second,' he once told an interviewer. He had to overcome, he had to push himself further, drive himself harder, because he has been afflicted since childhood with a weakness that would otherwise have held him back: scoliosis, an abnormal curvature of the spine. But the happier accident of his birth was that he was born a Jamaican.

So many elite sprinters come from Jamaica (Shelly-Ann Fraser-Pryce, Asafa Powell, Nesta Carter, Elaine Thompson, Veronica Campbell-Brown, to name just a few) that scientists have long wondered whether there is something in the air, something in the water. A study by researchers from the University of the West Indies found that the answer may be more down to what's in the earth. The high percentage of aluminium in the Jamaican soil can encode a gene known as ACTN3, which promotes the development of muscle fibres in a way that generates 'strong, repetitive contractions' – the rhythm of the runner in motion.

But there may be another, deeper reason why the race here is to the swift and strong. And that is race itself.

If we travel back in time, faster and faster, through the ages, to the middle of the sixteenth century, we will see the spiral of DNA echoing the curl of the ocean waves on a voyage from the shores of West Africa, across the raging Atlantic, to the tropical lull of the Caribbean. The cargo on board was human. When the ship docked, the survivors were yoked at the neck, shackled at the feet, and set free only to slave in the plantations, from four in the morning until sunset, hacking and harvesting sugar cane in the cloying heat. Those who survived the journey, those who survived the toil, were the strongest, the fastest, the hardiest. They went on to build the nation. To see a Jamaican athlete breaking the tape on the track today is to see the human spirit in surge, to taste the sweetness of victory, like the sugar in the marrow of the cane.

And what of us, here on the southern tip of that bloodline? What of the ships that came to our shores? What of our toil, our survival, our race to the finish? Let's contemplate that with the words of another great Jamaican ringing in our ears: 'Emancipate yourselves from mental slavery. None but ourselves can free our minds.' Bob Marley was saying that we alone must own responsibility for our freedom, for our redemption. But we can do that only if we remember what it means to be free.

The Gift of Having Nothing to Lose

I grew up in the township of Wattville, near Benoni, on the East Rand of Johannesburg, between the freeways and the mine dumps that always made me think of upturned bowls of yellow mealie pap. Oliver Reginald Tambo, then secretary general of the ANC, lived in Wattville in the 1950s before he went into exile. And he is buried here today, alongside his wife, Adelaide, in the shadow of the airport that now bears his name.

I was an in-betweener. I was born in 1985, when apartheid – the institution, if not the idea – was in its death rattle, on the cusp of the new dawn. I remember seeing soldiers in the township, in their dusty, malt-brown uniforms, cradling their rifles, eyeing us with a mixture of suspicion and fear. I remember seeing the armoured vehicles, lolling in the dips of the dirt roads like monsters rising from the swamp. I remember running, laughing, to join a big march in Dube Street, not knowing who was marching, or why.

But mostly I remember my grandmother's chickens. She kept them in her backyard. (What township Gogo didn't?) One day, the chicken coop was dirty, so she took the chicken out and tethered it by its leg to a tree. She left it there all day. Then, in the evening, she said, 'Vusi, go and untie the chicken and put it back in the coop.' So I undid the knot and slipped the rope off the chicken's scaly leg. It was free. But it just stayed there, frozen in place, resigned to its fate. I shooed it, pushed it, shouted and clapped it towards the coop. It feebly flapped its wings and clucked, but carried on scratching around in the narrow, invisible circle that had marked the limits of its world. Sometimes, when the rope has been cut we don't realise that the rope has been cut.

I hate the idea that I, because I am a black man, must blame somebody else for my disadvantage. I hate the notion that I, because I am a black man, must lack the means to take control of my own destiny. I can step outside the circle. I can fly. I think of those slaves, those survivors, wrenched from their villages and their families, forced into bondage in a faraway land. I think of the gift of speed and stamina and courage they would bequeath to the generations that followed.

What is our gift, as South Africans? It is the gift of opportunity, born from struggle. It is the gift of possibility, born from sacrifice. We come from deprivation, from lack, from want, from three and a half centuries of dominion and four decades of subjugation by a minority in our own land. We come from having nothing. That is our gift: that we have nothing to lose.

The Gift of Having Nothing to Lose

We have learnt over the years to live on very little, and that is why we are so good at dreaming of living on a lot. I must have been the biggest dreamer in all of Wattville. I remember the day my big dream swam into focus, from the blurry half-imaginings of my boyhood, into the crystal-clear colour and noise of unbridled ambition. That dream rode in on whitewall tyres, mag wheels and the roar of a V8 engine, competing with the boom-boom thump of a pounding bass. We stopped playing football and turned to look as the Ford Grenada, bottle-green, stirred up dirt and screeched to a halt. The music kept playing. The door opened, and a man stepped out from the driver's seat. We scoped him out, from his All Star shoes, to his leather trousers, to his silk shirt, to his Sportif hat, to his aviator sunglasses. He was all cool, all swagger, all money. His name was Mabaso, and I wanted to grow up to be exactly like him. Then I learnt what he did for a living. He jacked cars. I had the right dream, but the wrong role model.

Every South African township is a model of a mixed economy, from the big corporate chain stores to the spaza shops run from people's homes to the pavement hawkers selling fruit, sweets and peanuts on the street corners. But there is another economy, a sub-economy – one that thrives on illicit entrepreneurship, car jackings and robberies and petty theft. This is the vampire economy, so named because it sucks the life and blood from the system that is meant to sustain us. We are meant to work for a living, put in the hours, draw the reward that is commensurate with our endeavours. But it doesn't always work out that way.

On the subject of the underworld economy, somebody who was talking about black business, lamenting a string of failures, said to me, 'The trouble is that black people have not learnt how to organise.' Come on! Do you know what it takes to pull off a cash heist? Well, I don't personally, but let me hypothesise here. It takes military-level planning; in-depth knowledge; strategic thinking; split-second timing; carefully delegated, intensely coordinated teamwork; and the exact right amount of resources and equipment for the job. But, as a navy commander whom I worked with on a business project in the US once told me, 'No plan survives the first gunshot.' When hell breaks loose, all you can do is fall or run, with or without the cash in your hand. That's why I work in finance, equity, venture capital, entrepreneurship: there are fewer gunshots.

There was a gang in Wattville known as the Gerani Gang. I knew of them only by reputation, by street talk, by the fingers that pointed as cars drove by. Only years later, after I had left the township, did I discover where they took their name from – a menswear boutique called Gerani, which sells high-fashion, high-ticket, Italian-label shoes and clothing. Like them, we aspire higher, and there is nothing wrong with that. What is wrong is that we forget why we aspire.

For example, my brother came to me one day, excited, looking for brotherly advice. He was about to buy a car, and he knows I know cars. What should he buy? A V8? An SUV? A convertible? An Audi? A Merc? A Porsche, maybe? I stop him right there. 'Two things,' I say. 'One, God's been good, so it's not you. Two, and more importantly, it's not what you drive that matters. It's what drives you.' It sounds cheesy when I say it, but what I'm saying is, don't let the trappings of society define who you are.

The singer Thandiswa Mazwai, in her beautiful soaring voice, asks us, 'Have you forgotten the lineage that you come from? Have you forgotten the history, the tradition? Have you forgotten?' In the Western philosophical tradition, we say, '*Cogito, ergo sum*'. (I think, therefore I am). In the African tradition, we say, 'I am because you are.' But we forget that collective tradition. It is easier now for us to just say, as we strive, as we rise, as we succeed: 'I'. I live here,

I drive this, I do that, I have this, I want this, I want that. When you have nothing, you share everything. When you have everything, you keep everything to yourself. In the township, when you put a palisade fence around your house, it is a sign to everyone who passes by that you are going up in the world. You have something now, worth protecting, worth looking after. You have a barrier of spears between yourself and everybody else.

In township-taal, a palisade fence is called a 'stop nonsense' – as in, go away, don't bother me, 'stop your nonsense'. Where I stay now, on a secure golf estate, midway between Johannesburg and Pretoria, we don't have a stop nonsense around my house – but we do have one around the entire estate, electrified, with a boom gate, key code entry, ID verification and an always-manned control room at the entrance. When my mother comes to visit, she marvels at the greenery, the birdlife, the wide-open space. But she says: 'It's too quiet.' Her location is the location. For her, the noise, the buzz, the smell of food wafting in from the street, the clamour of people coming and going, popping in for a visit without calling to make an appointment . . . that is the poetry and the joy of living in that space.

I send my children to stay with my mother because I want

them to form relationships with people on the other side of the fence. I want them to grow up culturally and socially ambidextrous. At the same time, in their own home environment, on their own estate, it pleases me to know that when they see a black man, a neighbour, driving a Lamborghini, it's not something that should come as a shock. They don't need to stop playing their game to watch. The question we need to ask ourselves, when we think about these things is, why do so many black people leave the location? The answer is simple. They leave because the location reminds them of who they are and where they come from, not who they want to be and where they see themselves going. But the barriers of the mind remain.

When I go back to Wattville, I see shopping centres, new houses, bright-green grass on the soccer fields. But my mother still stays in the same house, goes to the same church, buys her beer from the same shebeen. She sends me to buy a six-pack. I ask, from the shebeen? She says, of course! But it's much cheaper at the supermarket down the road, I tell her. And what if somebody sees me? Somebody I know? What's that going to look like? 'Shhh,' she says. 'Go to the shebeen and buy me a pack.'

I grew up in two worlds, and I came to realise that both of them are based on a lie. I went to school in Wattville, and I was bright, smart, smooth-talking, always questioning, always answering, eager to please, eager to learn. I got pushed up three grades: accelerated, like a fast car. Our teacher, who also happened to be the principal, stood before our class one day. He picked a tennis ball off the table. He held it in his hand and began turning it slowly with his thumb, mimicking a revolution around the sun. 'The world is as round as a tennis ball,' he said, perfectly enunciating each syllable. It was the only thing he said in English during the entire lesson.

Then I went to high school in Benoni, a mixed-race Model C school, where English was the full-time language of instruction. I got moved down two grades. My fast car was suddenly going in reverse. On my first day, the geography teacher pointed at a globe on the table and said, 'The world isn't round. It's a geoid.' I almost fell off my chair. How could my principal have been so wrong? Or maybe my geography teacher had got it wrong. 'Geoid.' That means, when you break it down, that the earth is shaped like the earth. That's like saying water is a liquid because it's wet. But I grew to like my school, and I liked my fellow students, some of them a little more than others.

There was girl sitting a few rows away from me. She had a Greek surname. And she looked like a goddess. I asked her, eventually, when I caught up with her in the corridor one day, 'Will you go out with me?' To my amazement, she didn't say no. She said, 'I'll think about it.' The next day, I caught up with her again. 'Did you think about it?' I asked. 'Yes,' she said. And then she gave me her answer: 'No.' I made the mistake of asking her why. 'Because you're a kaffir,' she said.

The word hit me like a smack in the face. Nobody had ever called me that before. It spun me around, reeling me back across the great divide I foolishly thought I had crossed. When I recall this, it takes me back to the other world, back to Wattville, where every night, as a young boy, my mother would call me to undo her bra, because the clip had broken, so she had to tie it in a knot at the back. She couldn't afford to buy new underwear because she was sending us to school.

I think about that girl, the girl of my broken dreams, and I realise now that she was the one who was living in mental slavery. She was the one who was trapped in and by the past. I was free. I have learnt the truth about the world: that it isn't as round as a tennis ball, and it isn't shaped like itself. It is shaped the way we shape it, according to the way we see it, the way we mould it to our ambitions and our destiny.

I know the colour of who I am. I am a black man, running for my life, for my freedom, for opportunity born from struggle, possibility born from sacrifice. And I am running too, for my father, who never became what he hoped to be, and who never got to see what his children would one day become.

2

To Show Your Best at Your Worst

Tea and biscuits with Nelson Mandela;
the quest for the ultimate truth; and
the day my father walked to the tavern

I stood in the study, alone with the beating of my heart and the clink of a fine china teacup on a trembling saucer. I gazed out of the panoramic picture window at the rush of the fountain, and the fat koi in the fish pond, like darting rainbows in the ripple of the sun.

There were books all around me, an army of warriors bearing words that were mightier than the sword. I tilted my head up to read the titles. Tomes of the law, bound in leather and embossed with gold leaf; biographies of heroes, conquerors, world changers; classics of literature and philosophy; sacred handbooks of political and economic thought. But all I could think of at that moment was: I'm hungry.

VUSI

I had caught a taxi from Wattville early in the morning and walked the five kilometres from Joburg to the mansion in this quiet garden suburb. On a side plate on a silver tray that rested on the coffee table was an artful arrangement of Eet-Sum-Mor biscuits. The little squares resembled petals waiting to be plucked. We were often short of bread at home, but we were never short of shortbread. That was the one culinary luxury of my childhood, a teatime treat whose very name seemed to echo my desire, on the brink of adulthood, to make something more, more, more out of my life.

I reached for an Eet-Sum-Mor and put it to my mouth. It hovered in my hand. My mother, who had insisted I wear my school uniform, even though it was a school holiday, had sent me off to my meeting with three very strict instructions: look smart; sound intelligent; don't embarrass me.

Her great fear was that I would bring shame, not to myself, but to her as the head of the household and, by extension, to the street, the township, and the entire community with whom she had been sharing her motherly pride. If I crunched on the Eet-Sum-Mor, or even if I dipped it into my tea to soften it, there was a good chance that I would be caught with a spluttering mouthful of crumbs at the most inopportune moment, and I was already sweaty and nervous enough. So I put the biscuit back on the plate. I could hear footsteps coming down the corridor – a distinctive gait, sure and firm, with a slight after-shuffle. And then the voice, deep and rich, with a crackle of laughter as warm as a blazing log fire. He walked into the room. I knew from the photographs that he was a big man. I did not know that he was a giant. He stood and looked at me, and he opened his arms – they had the span of wings. 'My son,' he said. 'Come here.'

I instinctively touched the knot of my tie – look smart, sound intelligent, don't embarrass me – and I walked towards him with my hand outstretched. He brushed it away and embraced me in a hug. I could feel the tears welling up and it was too late to stop them streaming down my face. In that moment, he was my father, he was every father, he was the living link between a seventeen-year-old schoolboy and the history of his country, between the struggle and the dawn of freedom. 'Let's talk,' he said, and in the study of his home in Houghton, Nelson Rolihlahla Mandela gestured for me to take a seat at the coffee table.

I am a speaker. It's a big part of what I do for a living. I can stand on a stage anywhere in the world, and I can play an audience like an orchestra. I can sway them into contemplative silence; I can stir them into gusts of laughter; I can dazzle them with facts and figures that will shift the way they look at the world. I am schooled in the canons of rhetoric, the template for persuasive speech proposed by the Roman orator Cicero: invention, arrangement, style, memory and delivery. I am practised in the methods of persuasion, as elucidated by the Greek philosopher Aristotle: ethos, the appeal to ethics; pathos, the appeal to emotion; logos, the appeal to logic and reason. '*Loquor, ergo sum*', as one might put it in Latin. I speak, therefore I am.

Once, I delivered a talk in Parliament House, Canberra, Australia, after which the then prime minister, John Howard, said to me, 'You speak like a rock star.' So I took that to heart, and with all due grace and humility, used it to promote my business: Vusi Thembekwayo, the Rock Star of Public Speaking.

But on that day, in that chair, in that room, I was speechless. I knew that I would never be as powerful, as eloquent, as persuasive a speaker as the old man sitting next to me. I pictured him as the young lawyer, standing in the well of the courtroom defending his clients before the judge. I pictured him as Accused Number 1, standing in the dock defending the ideal for which he hoped to live, and for which he was prepared to die. I pictured him standing on the steps of Cape Town City Hall, on that February day in 1990, declaring himself to be not a prophet, but a humble servant of the people. And here he was, by my side, free at last from the demands of the Presidency, lifting the plate and insisting that I help myself to another Eet-Sum-Mor. How could I refuse?

'They tell me that you are a speaker,' he said, looking me straight in the eye. 'But you don't do much speaking.' He looked stern, disapproving, headmasterly. And then he chuckled, and he was Madiba once again. I had a question I wanted to ask him, just one question, so I could sound intelligent and justify my being in the same room as him, a schoolboy from Benoni High, whose only claim to fleeting celebrity was that he had won a prize at the World Championship of Public Speaking. It flattered me to know that Nelson Mandela knew of my achievement, that he knew I was a speaker, even if I was offering him very little evidence to prove it. But I wondered if he knew of my other story, and if that was the reason for the solace of the hug he had given me. I wondered if he knew the story of my father.

My father's name was Vusumuzi Nathaniel Thembekwayo. I bear a variant of the first part of his name: Vusi. My brother bears the other part: Muzi. My father said we would be joined by his name, we would each be a pillar of strength for the other. To him, fatherhood was the power of presence. There were five of us in the house, three biological siblings and two cousins, whom I call my brother and sister. My father would be there for us, a giant of a man with big, strong hands, butcher's hands, hands that would comfort you, pat you on the back, clasp your hand in his with a warmth and a force of life that could bind two hearts in one.

My father was a fighter. Not of the streets, but of the dojo, where he practised the Way of the Empty Hand, a form of full-contact karate called Kyokushin, which means 'the quest for the ultimate truth'.

Kyokushin karate was founded by a man named Masutatsu Oyama, a Korean-Japanese Sosai, or Great Master, who introduced the practice of tameshiwari – stone-breaking – into modern karate. Oyama reasoned that if he could smash blocks of stone into fragments, using his hands as sledgehammers, he could find the strength of body, mind and spirit to not only defeat his opponents, but to rise above his own fears and failings.

I would go with my father to the dojo, where we would train together, me shadowing his movements, the slow, lyrical turns, the sharp, sudden strikes, like a sapling in the shade of an oak. We would listen to the legends of the Great Master, how at the age of 23 he had retreated into the mountains, where he would shatter trees into splinters, meditate for hours under icy waterfalls, press twice his body weight hundreds of times a day. In later years, when he had long proved himself invincible in competition, he became famous for his ability to kill a bull with a single blow, a feat that earned him the nickname of Kami no te: the Hand of God.

Like my father, I have a black belt in Kyokushin, and the lesson I have learnt, the maxim that has stayed with me, is show your best at your worst. Follow through. Make the blows land. Carry on fighting, even when you are wounded and tired.

My father was a fighter. He left school with nothing more than a Junior Certificate, what used to be called a Standard Six. His father, my grandfather, who ran a small spaza shop and shebeen, believed that was enough schooling to make him a man. My father grew up in a house with ten siblings.

He was expected to go out and work. He found a job in a Kwikot factory, working on the production line, moulding metal into heat pumps and geysers. After work, he would go to the dojo, and then, when his father thought he was hanging out with friends, he would go to night school at St Anthony's Education Centre in Boksburg to study for his matric. It was the opposite of playing hooky.

He got his Senior Certificate, and a better job at General Electric, where he was granted the power to peer deep into the souls of his fellow workers and learn the secrets of their worth. He was a payroll clerk but he knew he was worth more than that, so there came a time – I was still very young – when he left his job and did what I would one day aspire to do as well: he became an entrepreneur. I never found out the nature of the business he started, but I do know that it was a disaster. We romanticise failure in the lore of the entrepreneur, as if it is a test of strength, a trial by combat, a valley of darkness that must be crossed on the pathway to the promised land. 'Fail again. Fail better!' we say, quoting Samuel Beckett. Or Thomas Alva Edison, who said that he had not failed 10 000 times, he had just found 10 000 ways that did not work. But the truth is, there is no romance in failure. All the more so when you have mouths to feed, when you are already living a life of struggle, when you have given up your steady job to chase a dream, only to watch it slowly crashing to the ground.

I remember sitting at home, watching my father reading the newspaper, with a pen in his hand, making red circles on pages dense with type. It was only much later that I realised he was looking for a job in the classified ads. He had bonded our house to start his business, and one of the things he bought was a Nissan Skyline, a shining symbol, perhaps, of his belief that the sky was the limit to what he could achieve. He couldn't keep up the payments, so the bank took the car. Then they wanted the house too. But my dad had a boss who wouldn't let the sheriff in. He was called Boss, his massive German shepherd, who would bark and show his fangs whenever the officer of the law arrived at the gate, papers in hand. As a safety measure, Mom sent us to live with our grandmother. We were a house divided. My father, the protector, the provider, with his big, strong hands, was now, in effect, an exile from his own family. My mother forbade us to see him, but we would sneak across to visit on the way home from school.

Then, one day, my grandmother turned 60. We had a party at her house, and of course, my dad was invited. It was good to see him. He looked happy. I was thirteen and eager to show him some of the moves I'd been practising – the kicks, strikes, and blocks that make up the ritual of the kata, the physical and spiritual lexicon of karate. He wasn't just my father. He was my Sensei, my teacher. We ate lunch, we sang 'Happy Birthday', we cut the cake. Then, because it had been a good party, the liquor ran out. My father offered to walk to the local tavern and pick some up. I knew his real motive. Even at the age of 41, he didn't want to be seen smoking in front of his mother. She disapproved of his habit. So did he, to tell the truth, but out in the street, he could light up and puff away without feeling too bad about it.

My father was a walk-and-talk kind of guy. A simple stroll to the shop could take him half the day, because he would stop and talk to people he knew, and stop and talk to people he didn't know, and wave at neighbours and at people in passing taxis. He wasn't famous, he was better than that: he was known. So we didn't worry when he took his time getting the liquor and making his way back to the house. Then we got worried. We called him on his cellphone. No answer. To this day, I don't know the truth of what happened. Nobody does, least of all the police, who never opened a case, never filed a docket, never made an arrest.

But the story seems to be that he walked into the shop, and someone took his cellphone, and there was a scuffle. He knew how to fight, but during the scuffle he was stabbed in the back. When he turned around, he was shot, nine times at close range.

That is not how I wish to remember my father. The abiding image, the imprint that is fixed in my mind, is of him sitting in the driver's seat of his car, not the Skyline, but a humble VW Golf, his hands gripping the wheel, as if he was ready to go on a journey, looking me in the eye and saying, 'Look after your mother, okay?'

In 2017 my wife gave birth to a son, our third child and second boy. I held him in my arms, my grip tender yet strong, in the way a father learns to do, because children are so fragile. He cried to the heavens. His name is Umnqobi; it means 'conqueror'. The conqueror of my heart, the conqueror of my soul. The line that connects us is the line that connects me to my father, and him to his father, and all of us to each other, because we all make the same cry when we are born.

That day, I sat at the coffee table with Nelson Mandela at my side, and I asked him, finally, if I could ask him a question. He seemed a little surprised to hear me speak, but he leaned in closer. I had thought about my question a lot. It wasn't the most original question in the world, nor was it the most profound. But I asked it anyway.

'Mr Mandela,' I said, 'what is your dream for South Africa?' He nodded to himself, his warm smile giving way to a look of deep, furrowed concentration. I had the feeling that he had thought a lot about this question too. And then he said, 'South Africans need a little bit of faith. My hope is that they can have just a bit more faith, in themselves and in this country.'

He spoke of hope, because hope works harder than a dream, because hope rolls up its sleeves and gets down to business. But he spoke of faith too, because faith is the ability to trust the unknown, to believe in the impossible, to see the invisible. And faith is knowing, whatever or whoever you may believe in, wherever you may come from or where you are going to, that the invisible keeps an eye on us too.

3
Shine, Vusi, Shine!

Identity and the mirror test;
my grandfather was never a whitey; and
the clever black who trended on Twitter

Growing up in our humble home, I was my mother's little sunbeam child. This I know to be true because, of all the boys and girls living under that roof, it was I who was the Chosen One. 'Vusi!' my mom would call from the kitchen, which served as the bridge of her battleship. 'Go and polish the stoep nicely now.'

That was my chore on the household roster, the toughest chore of them all: to coat the dull-grey cast of concrete with a layer of lipstick-red, the kiss of welcome for anyone who crossed the threshold that made our house a home. From the cupboard beneath the sink, I fetched the thick cloth and, with it, the tin with the face of the sun on top, the crown of spiky rays, the dimples, the lips curled into a smile that always struck me as smug. And with good reason, because life always felt more bright and shiny when I held a tin of Sunbeam in my hand. I gave the lid a twist, and the polymers hit the air with a puff, the molecules bonding into memory with the waxy, intoxicating smell of . . . what was it? Beeswax? Petroleum? No.

From where I sit now, even after all these years, I recognise it for what it was – the Smell of Pride. On the stoep, I would get down on my hands and knees, I would dab the cloth into the Sunbeam and I would buff, buff, buff, in small circles, then big circles, then zigzags and stripes, as I painted my masterpiece in polish.

But you know mothers. They expect and demand more from us because we are their masterpieces in the making. My mom would come outside to see how I was doing. It would be hot, I would be sweating, the sun shining its sunbeams on my face, me shining the stoep with Sunbeam. 'Make it shine, Vusi,' Mom would urge me. 'Make it shine!' She would stoop down and run a finger across the gloss, the captain of the ship conducting her inspection. 'Mandela would be proud to sit on this stoep,' I would say, pausing for a moment to admire my handiwork. But, no, if it didn't pass the mirror test, it didn't pass the Mom test. I had to be able to see myself reflected in the shine. I sighed and got back to buffing.

I couldn't understand at the time why a stoep had to be polished to such a gleam – and ours went all the way around the house, like the board under a cake, to the back, where the dog slept. After all, it was designed to be walked on, by family, friends and neighbours, the traffic of a community coming and going, and all the footprints and shoe prints would eventually dull the dazzle, and I would have to get down on my hands and knees with my tin of Sunbeam all over again.

But now I know why. My mother wanted me to look deeper than the surface, deeper than the Sunbeam. She wanted me to reflect, through sweat and toil, on who I was, where I had come from, who I could grow up to be. Shine, Vusi, shine.

So here I am again, still hard at work, still polishing away. Only, now my buffer zone is the driveway of my home on the golf estate, and I am Simonizing the bonnet of my metallic-black V8 to a sheen. In the background I can hear the playful laughter of my children, and it strikes me that they will most likely never be tasked with Sunbeaming a stoep, just as I, when I was their age, was never called on to herd cattle into a kraal. The threads that connect us to our ancestors grow more slender with each passing generation, until all that is left is memory, spirit and the blood that courses through our veins.

As I catch sight of my reflection in the black metallic burnish of my car, I wonder if my grandfather would recognise me, if he would see himself in me, in this idyllic estate where he wouldn't even have been allowed to sit at a table in the restaurant when he was my age. He was born the wrong colour in the wrong country at the wrong time. In 1978, two years after Soweto went up in flames, one year after Steve Biko was manacled, naked, in the back of a police vehicle and driven to his death in Pretoria, my grandfather opened a small spaza shop in his home township in KwaZulu-Natal.

In that same year, in Stellenbosch, a chartered accountant and retail operations executive by the name of James Wellwood 'Whitey' Basson set off on an acquisition trail that led to the purchase of a small Western Cape chain of grocery stores called Shoprite. Today Shoprite is the largest food retailer on the African continent. It is worth more than R118 billion, and every minute of every day – and when I tell people this from the stage, I can see their eyes widening and their fingers tallying up the numbers – it turns over a million rand. A million rand a minute. I often wonder, what if my grandfather had been given an equal chance? What if he had been able to go to university and get an education? What if he had been able to open up shop wherever he pleased? What if he had been born a whitey? I know the answer to all these what-ifs. I can see it clearly as I polish away the layers of history. The answer is me.

I can live and work and wander, and bring up my kids wherever I choose. I am not constrained or held back by a law that says I am lesser than or other. And yet, as a young black South African, having freely made my choices, I know too that there is one way in which I am not yet free. I am not free from what other people think of me. Listen to me speak. Hear my voice: I have trained it to be clear and strong, to carry to the back of the hall, to soar into the peaks and whisper in the valleys. I used to stammer as a schoolchild; my ideas would trip and stumble on the path to being spoken. That is why I chose to become a debater, a speaker. I wanted my ideas to be heard, to shape the air around me into a bridge between people, cultures and nations. I expect people to charge at me on that bridge, to tell me how and why my ideas are wrong. Speech is freedom. But listen to my accent too. It is not the accent of KwaZulu-Natal, the green and hilly land of my ancestors. It is not the accent of Wattville, the gritty township where I grew up. It is the accent of transition, moulded by a fusion of class and cultures on the cusp between apartheid and democracy.

It is known colloquially, after the first integrated state schooling system of the new era, as a Model C accent. And when people tell you that you speak with a Model C accent, they never mean it as a compliment. It is a pejorative remark, a code word for accusing you of having allowed your blackness to be bleached. It is perceived and received as an affectation, the implication being that you have been affected by your intersection with the default culture of the once white-only suburbs, and the bleach has seeped into your brain. 'White people love Vusi, because they love the way Vusi speaks.' I heard that comment from a radio deejay once, and it made me laugh. But I don't speak for white people. I speak for myself. This is what I sound like. This is who I am. I am Vusi, who was taught to shine. Every time I open my mouth, I give away my identity but, at the same time, I claim it back. When I stand on a stage in Joburg or Stockholm or Dubai or Cape Town or Las Vegas or Barcelona, do people listen to me for what I say, or for the way that I say it? My hope is that it is the former.

If I work on my biceps, if I tone my upper body, if I spend an hour or two a day lifting and spinning and running on the spot at the gym, people will say, 'Vusi, you're looking good!' But if I were to spend an equal amount of time flexing my consonants and vowels, sharpening my diction, stretching my vocabulary, then, in the view of some people, like that deejay, I would not be working out, I would be selling out. I would be stepping out, defiantly, from the series of categories to which I have been confined, the interlocking nesting boxes of my destiny and my identity.

Who am I, this Vusi who looks back from the Sunbeam on the stoep, the Simoniz on the bonnet? When it comes to the question of our identity, we peel away the layers by revealing who we are, where we come from, what we do. That is how we get to the core. It is the way we trace our histories and forge connections, seeking the common ground on which we can build our personal and professional relationships. So, I am Vusi, short for Vusumuzi – 'the builder of the home' – from Wattville via KZN and Swaziland. I am black, male, a millennial, South African, a speaker, a business owner, a venture capitalist, an entrepreneur. All of these things are a part of me; none of them make up the whole of me.

We need to understand that identity is a fluid construct. It flows like a river. We don't stand on the bank and watch it rushing by; we jump right in and see where it will carry us. When we introduce ourselves to each other, as coming from Wattville or Soweto or Alex, we say that with pride, because those places are true to our identity; they shaped us. But why do we allow our sense of who we are to be framed by places that were designed to confine us, to keep us from becoming citizens of the world? My identity is not pegged to where I come from. It is liberated by where I want to go.

In the same way, my identity is not just framed by the colour of the face I see in the mirror, a poster child for what Twitter calls 'black excellence', always accompanied by an emoji of a pair of black hands clapping. If I am going to be excellent, let me be excellent for what I have done, not because I happen to have it done it while being black. Why must we classify excellence by its colour, as if it lies on a Pantone scale, with white, the absence of colour, as the benchmark at its centre? Why, when you are black and successful, do you run the risk of being labelled, even if only behind your back, as 'Ingama', which means 'white'?

If you are black and successful, then you are seen to be white, because in our minds, success is seen to be white, not black. If this is true, it would explain why, when a black person succeeds, we go out of our way to find reasons to explain their success. It is because they sold out; it is because they went to this or that school; it is because they have connections in high places; it is because they speak with a twang in their voice. We will find a thousand reasons, but we fail to home in on the one that matters the most, the simplest, the most likely: they are a success because they are good, maybe even better than anybody else, at what they do. I never heard my father talking about excellence as a black thing or a white thing. But I often heard him talking about what it took to achieve excellence: sweat, honesty, integrity, hard work, respecting your elders. He espoused the idea that you had to go out looking for your success in life, that it wouldn't come and meet you if you sat at home waiting. But first, you had to find yourself. He meant that philosophically, in a Zen kind of way, but looking back now, I think my mother meant exactly the same thing when she sent me out to shine the stoep.

VUSI

My dad kept our dog chained up during the week because, in a township, you don't want a big German shepherd named Boss running around biting people. On the weekend, my dad would take the dog out for a run. Boss, let off the leash, would bolt into the wind, barking at the air, darting wildly this way and that, pausing only to sniff intently at the trees and the grass. But he wasn't free. He had just been freed. That is us too, as black South Africans – as long as we continue to think of ourselves as freed people, rather than as free people, we will continue to be chained in our minds. The system of oppression that we fought and defeated no longer lives in law, but it lives on inside us like a virus, whenever we look down on someone as less than or other. This is the greatest victory of apartheid: it taught black South Africans to see themselves as a cursed generation, as hewers of wood and drawers of water, to use the biblical phrase so loved of Verwoerd. Even today the ghost of that self-image lingers on, not just in the way we look down on each other, but in the way we look up and tear each other down. In Australia, this practice is so commonplace that it has a name – tall poppy syndrome. The poppy that rises above the field must be snipped down to size, in the name of egalitarianism. But in a meritocracy, that is a false premise. Egalitarianism does not mean that everyone must be equal. It means that everyone must be granted an equal chance to prove that they can be better than anyone else. That they can shine brighter.

On a cloudless night, when you gaze up at the heavens, and your head spins at the vastness of just our little portion of the Milky Way, it is always the brightest stars that will command your attention – Venus, Jupiter, Acrux. But, as any astronomer will tell you, these are not by any means the brightest of the celestial objects that can be seen with the naked eye. They just have better stories to tell: Venus, the evening star, first to rise when the sun slips from the sky; Jupiter, the giant among planets; Acrux, the steadfast anchor of the Southern Cross. We are drawn to them because they dazzle us. It's just a matter of perception.

In the world of business too, we look to the stars for meaning. In marketing, we use a concept called the Net Promoter Score, which is a way of measuring a customer's willingness to recommend a company's products or services to others. Based on their answer to a single survey question, respondents are classified as promoters, loyal enthusiasts who will keep buying and refer others; passives, who are satisfied but unenthusiastic; and detractors, unhappy customers who can damage a brand through negative word of mouth.

Let's assume the brand in question is South Africa itself. I'll tell you what we don't have here: we don't have passives. We are never neutral or lukewarm. We shout and argue about politics, about sport, about business, about culture, about race, about language, about jobs, about money. We even shout and argue about shouting and arguing, as I discovered for myself when I tweeted, using the hashtag #ThingsIHate: 'People who think they can debate with you on Twitter ... meanwhile we are not even in the same tax bracket.' Yoh!, as we say on Twitter. I thought I was merely being mischievous, deliberately igniting a hot-button proposition to get the sparks flying, as one might do to warm up the rhetorical muscles during a debating competition. You challenge yourself by deliberately taking a contrarian position, to see how well you can perform at a remove of 180 degrees.

Of course I'm covering for myself here, but let's just say on that day, as I became a trending topic on Twitter, that I didn't even manage to put my theory to the test. I didn't get a word in edgeways. Which is just as well, because who wants to butt into the conversation when you're being called a 'clever black' with a Model C accent? And that was just one of the gentler insults. And yet, if clever and black are aspects of my identity, along with the accent, I'll take them.

Among the detractors, the haters, the shouters, I'll be a net promoter of myself, shining my own image, polishing my perceptions of who I am and what I can do. Because that's the job for which I was chosen and, let me tell you, when you're down on your hands and knees with your Sunbeam on the stoep, trying to pass the mirror test, the last thing you want to do is get on the wrong side of my Ma.

4
The Lie of the Land

The great fallacy of golf;
the law of the African mother; and
the difference between land and space

It is early in the morning and the sun has just risen from the ruffled blanket of the hills when I step onto the terrace and cast an eye over the lie of the land. For a moment, I feel like the captain of a ship, standing on the prow, the wind whipping the waves to carry me to the green and pleasant shore. The land stretches like a carpet before me, cropped and cross-hatched in shades of light and dark. At its fringes the wild grass grows, harbouring the dangers that lurk in terra incognita, the unknown land. The undulating terrain is pocked by patches of golden sand, raked like a Zen garden, smoothed over and left in wait for the missiles that will plummet from the sky and the nub-soled shoes that will scatter the carefully arranged grains.

The first round of golf is about to begin. But I won't be playing. It took me a while to figure out the great fallacy of golf, which is that the object of the game is not so much to slam and drive and gently nudge a little dimpled ball along the fairway into a hole in the ground, as it is to take a long, slow walk in the company of people who can help you go a fair way in your business.

But the truth is, people who already know each other will play golf together, but people will not play a round of golf to get to know each other. On top of that, for me at any rate, it is hard work, and if you get stuck too often in the bunker or the rough, with the sand stinging your eyes or the weeds tangling at your feet, bang goes your prospect of doing a deal.

So, as an exercise in networking, golf is nowhere near as useful as, say, flying business class. Economy is a combat zone, with every square centimetre of territory a contested space. You're fighting for the armrest, scrambling for the overhead locker, battling with your knees to keep the passenger in front of you from ramming you into the passenger behind. But when you're in Business, you're in business.

The other day, as I slide onto my seat, I notice that my seat mate looks familiar. I have a moment of mind-racking, flipping through the back files of my memory, the magazine covers, the TV interviews, the annual reports. And then . . . jackpot. She's a philanthropist, an entrepreneur, a company director, a frequent and fearless commentator on good governance and the state of the economy. 'Hi, my name is Vusi,' I say as I buckle up. By the time we hit cruising altitude, my tray table is down, and I'm leafing through a sheaf of papers, making a note or circling a number here and there. It's a shareholders' agreement. 'Business?' asks my seat mate, giving me the side-eye. It's a rhetorical question. I nod, with a smile. Then she asks: 'Is it BEE?' I'm all serious for a moment. 'I don't believe in BEE,' I say. Her eyes widen, as if the captain has just activated the fasten-your-seatbelt sign. I tell her I'm a venture capitalist. I finance small and growing businesses. 'Ah,' she says, 'that's interesting . . . Tell me more.'

By the time we touch down in Cape Town, I'm in her contacts and she's in mine, and who knows where it might lead from there one day? If we'd been playing golf, I'd probably still be swivelling my hips and worrying about my backswing.

But this is not to suggest that I have anything against golf courses per se. On the contrary, as I stand here on the terrace overlooking the golf estate where I stay, two things occur to me. One, no matter how far I may move away from my childhood home, I'll always think of a terrace as a stoep; and two, the sight of this golf course pleases me. It stands for neatness, order, a sense of calm and control amid the chaos of the world.

But that is the lie of the land. Because the truth is, the land we live in, the land we live on, isn't calm and controlled: it's fiercely contested. Here in South Africa, if you dig a spade into the earth, whether to plant a seed or lay the foundation for a building, you open a wound of history, you cut into more than three and a half centuries of conquest, colonialism, dispossession, dispersal, dislocation. The earth lies screaming.

On my way from Joburg, I spotted this poster on a lamp post: 'Land: Blacks own 1.2%'. Further on, when I passed by the dip of the valley on the skirts of the freeway, I glanced at the city of brick and clay and tin. There were houses jutting out haphazardly from a patch of veld that would be too small to accommodate even a single hole of golf.

How big is a golf course, I wondered? Turns out it's about 150 acres, or 60 hectares, for a full eighteen-hole course.

How many dwellings could you fit on that golf course, if you were to – and here I use a phrase that has become part of the everyday discourse on social media and political party platforms – take back the land?

Back at the golf estate, I scroll through a document titled 'Sustainable Medium-Density Housing' compiled by the Development Action Group, a South African NGO. Here I learn that medium-density housing means approximately 40 to 100 dwelling units per hectare of land.

So, erring on the side of moderation, that means you could comfortably fit 50 small semi-detached dwellings on a hectare. Multiply that by the area of a golf course, and you've got 3 000 dwellings. Assume, once again on the basis of a conservative estimate, that each dwelling houses four people, on average. That means you could accommodate at least 12 000 people where now the electric carts hum and the four-balls amble across the green. But wait. I'm not suggesting you try this. For one thing, it would be against the code of conduct of the estate, and that is a document that is watched over and enforced with more vigilance than the Constitution. Just try playing loud music after 10:30 pm, and see where that gets you.

But I also have a few questions about taking back the land. They are: what land? Where? For what purpose? And then, what happens?

Let me begin with the commonplace notion that the land was taken away from its original inhabitants, shortly after those unfurled sails appeared on the horizon, and the *Reijger*, the *Dromedaris* and the *Goede Hoop* dropped anchor off Table Bay, and those men in their strange clothes set foot on the golden shore. But I want to argue against this common myth. The land wasn't taken away. It is still there, every square centimetre of it, and it will be for billions of years, at least until the sea rises or a comet falls from the sky. What was taken away, instead, was what the land means to us. Our sense of pride in it, our sense of belonging to it, our sense of being connected to it, in heart and soul, across the generations, were whipped away from beneath our feet, in the way that a magician will whip a cloth from a table and leave the crockery standing.

What we need to do now is take back what the land means, and make it mean even more. The land – scoop it up and let it run through your fingers, tread on it with your bare feet, follow its sweep to the endless horizon – stands for prospect, possibility, the hope of harvest. It stands for something bigger than itself. That doesn't mean, suddenly, when the day comes, that we will all be granted a packet of seeds and a piece of turf with our name on it. The farmers will carry on tilling and ploughing, toiling away at the toughest job under the sun. But for the rest of us, the world has turned. We have moved beyond the Grand Agrarian Revolution, beyond the theory of Keynesian economics, according to which – let me step up to the whiteboard for a moment – land, labour and capital are the essential factors of production in an economy. Today technology is shifting the way capital is used, so that land, to a certain extent, has become zero-rated. It is no longer the critical input it used to be. Where does Apple own land? What land does Google hold dominion over in the 21st century? It is the landscape of your mind, in which you plant ideas, and upon which you build the property of your intellectual capital, that counts most today.

But let's get back down to earth for a moment. Sure, you can knock on my door and say, 'Vusi, are you with us? We're going to take back the land!' Great, I'll say, I'm in. You want me to show up, I'll be there. I'll be flying the flag, shouting the slogans, chasing the landowners off their ill-gotten land. But in the midst of it all, don't be surprised if I turn around and say, 'Wait, what is the end goal here? What are we hoping to achieve?'

I want to knock on your door one day and tell you that we don't need the land to realise our dreams, to make a success of our lives, to generate vast amounts of wealth. We don't need the land to construct new systems, new classes of assets, new ways of thinking and working and looking at the world. We need to find a new reason for our existence. The horse, when the motor car was invented, was suddenly just a horse without a cart; it needed to find a new reason to be. Likewise, we cannot continue to rely on assets backed by land as our ticket to the game. The land is a physical element, a presence to which we are bound by gravity, birthright and ancestral memory. But what if we were to rise above it, to reclaim our pride, our belonging, our connection, by reaching instead for the stars?

The earth ties us down. It zones and confines us. Boundless imagination, on the other hand, is what will set us free. There is a difference between land and space. They are not the same thing. People need to be given space, to self-express, to self-create, to self-explore, to try and to fail and to try all over again. They need to be given space to get lost in their own mind. That is where art, philosophy and entrepreneurship begin. But I guess you can't put up a political party poster that says: 'Take back the space!' – because the space will always be there for the taking.

My grandfather's name was David Thembekwayo. The legend in our family was that he was a landowner, with vast tracts to his name in the green and rolling hills of Mpumalanga, close to his ancestral home in Swaziland. He didn't do anything with the land: he didn't farm on it, build on it, let it or subdivide it. He owned it, and that was enough. It was tribal land, passed down through the generations, and the story is that it was eventually sold back into the land-claims process. But I can't say for sure. You know what it's like when you're still a child, and you're listening to the talk at the dinner table, and you don't understand what's going on, but from the tone and the raised voices, you can tell it's big, serious adult business. That's what it was like between my father and my grandfather. My grandfather was uKleva – too clever for his own good. He would always find a way to rig the system, to work it in his favour. He would buy furniture on hire purchase, on the never-never, and when the collectors came to repossess it, he would chase them away with an axe or a sjambok. His wife, Esther, meanwhile, would work hard in the kitchen all day, making food to sell to the men in the factories. My father resented that. He saw it as an abdication of responsibility by my grandfather. Hence, the shouting at the table. I didn't let it bother me, because I grew up in that little house in Wattville with a gift that money couldn't buy: the gift of space.

I had space to learn in the books that I read, I had space to play in the streets and the parks, I had space to dream of the bigger, brighter world that lay beyond Wattville. We lived in a corner house, and right opposite was the railway. I would stand outside and watch the trains go by, carrying coal one minute, livestock the next, human beings the next. I would wave to the driver and I would wonder, always, where they were going. And overhead, in the clear blue sky, I would see a jet plane forming contrails, soaring upwards from the runway just down the road. I had the sense, just by standing still, that the world around me was in motion, restless, questing, dynamic.

I wanted to go places too. But it was difficult: whenever I had to leave the place of my roots to go to the big city, Joburg, I could feel the fear in my bones, the shadow over my shoulder, the coldness of concrete and glass and steel that blocked out the sun. If you grow up in a small town, you are like a fish in a fishbowl. The fish doesn't know it's in a fishbowl; it doesn't know that it belongs in the ocean. That small-town thinking stays with you for life. Either it sets you up as a dreamer, driven to break free from your confines, to follow the rails or ride the clouds to the big time, or it narrows your view of the world, it hems you in, it makes you perpetually suspicious of city folk and their motives.

I see these different kinds of thinking in business all the time. People who have grown up in a privileged background, who come from spaces that are vast and expansive, have an innate sense that there is more than enough room for everybody in their plans. They start their thinking with an open map, a blue-sky vision: 'Just how big do you want this to be?' they'll ask. Whereas, when I do business with people from a disadvantaged background, they are often predatory and insular in the way they assume and consume power. They worry that if they open up space for others, there will be less space for them to occupy, so they charge in, lock others out of position, and accumulate everything in their path. It's built into their way of thinking: 'The more you have, the less I am going to have.' So they take it all.

Space. It all comes down to space. Hundreds of years ago, when the ships came, they were driven by the will of the wind and the philosophy of manifest destiny: the belief that the colonialists on board were doing God's work, that they had the heavenly right to cross the wild ocean and lay claim to whatever they found on the faraway shore. It is time now for us to make our destiny manifest too.

The faraway shore is the future. We travel there on the wings of our energies, our ideas, our ambitions. But we have to start somewhere. As I stand here on the terrace of the golf estate, watching the sun cast a glow on the clouds, I think to myself, there is nothing of me in this place. Culturally, it is neutral, clinical, devoid of personality. The only thing we have in common here, me and all the other residents, is the golf course and the code of conduct. Those are the things that bind us, that make us a community. But I chose to stay here because I wanted a place where my children could play, where they could step out of the door and run and be free.

Ultimately, that is all we want, all we really need from the land. A little patch of it, bonded to our hearts and souls and the memories we make. A little patch we can call home.

5

To Lead is to Learn to Command the Silence

The music of silence; how the Reverend Dr Martin Luther King winged his dream; the four-second rule of spoken communication; and the things you hear when you shut up and listen

The lights of the venue fade. In the whispering darkness, I hear the first notes of a fanfare, a deep electronic hum that seems to be rising from the inner core of the earth. It builds to a crescendo, unleashing a volley of piercing green laser beams, as the ghost voice booms: 'Ladies and gentlemen, please welcome your keynote speaker for today—'

That's my cue. I sprint in from the wings (that's why you'll find me at the gym every morning at six o'clock) and I look out at the faces as the wave of applause subsides. 'Hi,' I say, 'I'm Vusi.' Then I do something that allows me to hold the crowd in the palm of my hand, to command their emotions, to keep them not just engaged, but mesmerised. I just stand there and I say nothing. Tick-tick-tick. You could wring the tension from the air, like sweat from a towel. I can see frowns appearing on the faces now, a growing sense of concern: have I forgotten my presentation? Have I had a sudden attack of nerves? Have I lost my way in the deepest thickets of thought?

No. What I am doing is wielding the power of one of the most effective tools in the arsenal of the public speaker. The power of . . . silence. When you grow up with a stammer, as I did – with your thoughts as clear as crystal, but then splintering into fragments when you try to turn them into words – you quickly realise how precious a gift speech is, and all the more so when you wrap it up in silence.

It is in the pauses, the intervals, the spaces between the words, that the meaning of what you are saying sinks in. To listen to a good speech, whether from a pulpit or a podium, whether off-the-cuff or seared into memory, is to hear a kind of music, not just in the register, the lilt, the cadence and the rhythm, but in those moments when there are no words to be heard, when all you can hear is the enveloping silence.

The great American jazzman Miles Davis once said that silence is the real music; the notes that surround it are merely the frame. You can hear this – or more accurately, you can sense it – most explicitly on a track called 'What You Say', from his *On the Corner* album, where he experimented with a collision of jazz, funk and rock that blares with the chaotic energy of a planet being born. Then, every now and again, the onslaught suddenly stops, and in the lingering silence that ensues you can hear the real music. It's almost as if Miles wants to drive us headlong towards that epiphany. Even his famous muted trumpet falls completely mute, and yet we can hear it drifting in the echo of the void. That same principle, of absence as a form of presence, applies to speaking in public. 'Don't speak unless you can improve the silence,' advised Argentinian author Jorge Luis Borges.

But sometimes, the silence can improve the way we speak. Listen to the way a southern Baptist preacher addresses his congregation, more than a quarter of a million strong, on a hot summer day in Washington, DC. It is August 1963. He is the keynote speaker at the March on Washington for Jobs and Freedom, a milestone in the history of the civil rights movement, and his text for the occasion has been set in stone; a draft has already been distributed to the media. But, as he nears the end of his speech, weaving in themes of slavery and emancipation and the 'sweltering summer' of discontent that has spread across many American cities, he reads the mood of the crowd and switches from his prepared monologue, like a train deviating onto a different track. He skips across a section that in retrospect seems dry and leaden, a concluding call to community action, and he ignites his speech instead with the spark of a rhythm, a fast train stopping at the stations of injustice, where citizens had been denied the right to vote on account of the colour of their skin. 'Go back,' he says. 'Go back to Mississippi, go back to Alabama, go back to South Carolina, go back to Georgia, go back to Louisiana . . .'

Then, from out of the crowd, rising from the ripples of applause, he hears the call of the gospel singer Mahalia Jackson, who had earlier warmed up the gathering with a pair of rousing spirituals. Now, sitting nearby, she shouts, as if swayed by the Holy Spirit during a sermon: 'Tell them about the dream, Martin!'

He looks up, glances across at the singer, and slowly slides the guiding gospel of his document across the lectern. And then the Reverend Dr Martin Luther King Jr, his voice reverberating with a new-found fervour, tells them, in words that carry across the ages, across the generations: 'I have a dream.'

At the MyGrowthFund offices in Grayston Drive, Sandton.

In the backyard of my childhood home
in Wattville, Benoni, in 1988.

'But there was something else that set me apart,
an aspect of my being that was a source of deep pride,
as much as a point of persistent pressure.
I was the black guy in the room.'

Top: My official school picture in 2002, when I was in Grade 11 at Benoni High.

Bottom: At the National Public Speaking Competition in 2001 with Tarquin Phillip, left, and Yasmin Motara.

'Money is a fleeting gift. If you spend it, it's as if you never had it. If you keep it, it's as if you'll never need it. But if you trade it, if you buy something to sell something, then you're on your way to unlocking the secret of what money really means.'

With fellow participants at the English-Speaking Union competition in 2002 in the UK.

'I've always been big on dreams. I don't want to fly Business Class; I want to own the airline. I don't want to go on holiday; I want to own the island. I don't want to drive a Porsche; I want to own the factory.
I don't want to be a survivalist. I want to be a thrivalist.'

'If clever and black are aspects of my identity, along with the accent, I'll take them. Amidst the detractors, the haters, the shouters, I'll be a Net Promoter of myself, shining my own image, polishing my perceptions of who I am and what I can do. '

To Lead is to Learn to Command the Silence

His eyes have left the page now, and he is looking out across the teeming masses, sometimes gazing heavenwards, and you can see his mind working, improvising, plucking riffs and refrains from the air. The power of this most celebrated section of his most celebrated speech lies as much in what he does not say as in what he does, in the dramatic pauses, like the *shhh* of a freight train shunting, that crown his vision with an aura of poetry. He is speaking slowly, deliberately, at a pace of about 95 words a minute, compared to the standard conversational rate of between 140 and 160. 'I have a dream,' he says, and he pauses. 'That one day on the red hills of Georgia,' and he pauses again, for longer still, 'the sons of former slaves and the sons of former slave owners will be able to sit down at the table of brotherhood. I have a dream . . .' He is splitting up his sentences, sowing them in the furrows of memory, and it is that phrase, spoken eight times during his speech, that takes root and blooms to harvest. Spoken at a normal rate, the rate of simply reading from a page, the words 'I have a dream' would have lost their impact, their impetus, the momentum that drove the phrase into mythos and meaning. In the silence that frames it, we can hear the music.

Not all of us are able to speak the way Martin Luther

King Jr spoke. But all of us can learn to harness the power of silence. Silence gives us a pause to reflect, to absorb, to weigh up our judgement and measure our responses, to turn our thoughts inward or to set them adrift to the furthest reaches of the universe. But, mostly, silence gives us the space we need to listen. It sharpens our senses, it puts us on high alert, it creates an exquisite tension between anticipation and revelation. We think of oratory as the ability to project, to persuade, to galvanise an audience with words and phrases that ring like a hammer on an anvil. But, in truth, the speaker who is best able to do that will be the speaker who has best learnt how to command the silence in between. There are moments when I am on stage – I call them moments of silence – when I am saying something, making a point, telling a story, contextualising or elucidating a snippet of data, and suddenly, slam, fullstop. There is silence.

I look out into the audience, and no one is shifting in their seat, no one is staring at their phone, no one is whispering to the person sitting next to them. Everyone is completely engaged, wrapped up in the tick-tick-tick of the fleeting moment. As a speaker, you plan for those moments, those little rest stops in the notation of your speech. If you play them right – and there is a fine line between an awkward silence and a silence rich with meaning – you can create chasms of contemplation across which the audience can leap into understanding.

But here too, there is a paradox that comes into play – the paradox of silence, which states that there is no such thing as silence. If you look at the musical score for a composition titled 4'33" by American avant-garde composer John Cage, you will see that it consists entirely of rest stops: 137 bars, equating to four minutes and 33 seconds of complete silence.

At first it looks like a parody of a real piece of music, especially when you watch it being played in concert. The maestro, brushing the tails of his tuxedo out of the way, takes his seat at the grand piano, turns the page of the score-sheet, peers at it through his glasses, picks up a stopwatch and presses the button, and shuts the lid of the piano with his other hand.

This ritual carries on for three movements, and it is conducted in all earnest, because the point of it is to make us pay attention to the quiet, and to realise that the silence that surrounds us is never complete. Someone in the auditorium coughs; a chair scrapes on the floor; the stopwatch ticks; the lid slams; there is a shuffle, a hum, a high-pitched electric twirl, a flapping of paper, a car driving by in the distance. Forced to listen, to open our ears and minds anew, we become acutely aware of silence as a colour, a texture, a kaleidoscope, a landscape in itself. The same applies when we seek to escape the bustle and pressures of the city, and we hear the music of the bush or the ocean, the chirruping of crickets, a faraway roar, a rustle in the grass, the hooting of an owl, the rush of the waves, the slither of the sand. That's why we often struggle to fall asleep in the sanctuary of nature: the silence is too loud.

In the world of business too, the world of hard talk and fast decisions, silence can speak volumes. If you are negotiating with someone, over price or terms, and they suddenly fall quiet and just sit there looking at you, it can be very tempting to fill the silence, to talk yourself down from the high ground, losing your footing in a rockfall of things you never meant to say. This is because, for most of us, it is so difficult to read the silence: it is like a cloak your adversary puts on to conceal their true thoughts and intentions. Does the silence mean that they've run out of steam or patience? Does it mean that they're feeling bored or sullen?

Does it mean, deep inside, that they're thinking about it? Or does it mean that they're on the very verge of conceding, and here you are, rambling in where angels fear to tread? There is an old legal maxim that says, '*Qui tacet consentire videtur*', which means, 'He who is silent is taken to agree'. To say nothing, ergo, is to say yes. But here's the problem with this proposition, as rooted as it may be in jurisprudence. It's tough to say nothing. It goes against the grain of our nature as a loquacious social species. We like to talk.

Sometimes, between lovers, friends, partners, comrades, old acquaintances, silence can be an eloquent and embracing form of communication. We know each other well enough to leave certain things unsaid. But in more general company, too much silence can leave us feeling uneasy, anxious, even disturbed. How much is too much? Count to four. Four seconds. That's it. In 2011, a team of Dutch researchers conducted a series of experiments on what are known as disaffiliative disfluencies, or breaks in the natural flow of conversation in a social setting. Anyone who has ever been to a dinner party where the buzz of chatter suddenly, mysteriously comes to a stop, and all you hear is the tinging of cutlery on plates, and the sound of wine being too loudly imbibed, will be familiar with this phenomenon. Okay, I'm not, because my dinner party friends never stop talking. But, according to the research, which was published in the *Journal of Experimental Social Psychology*, a silence of four seconds or more can make the conversation feel 'significantly less pleasant', partly because it induces in us a primal sense of ostracism from a group. Our evolutionary survival mechanism kicks in: we feel threatened, rejected, abandoned, so we sit there, desperately trying to think of something to say, to work our way back into the circle, and then of course everyone starts talking at once, and the silence is mercifully broken.

However, in a corporate setting you can use that four-second rule to your advantage. If you are talking to a group and you feel a restlessness in the air, or you notice people toying with their phones, don't slam your fist on the table and yell at them to listen up. Just shut yourself up, and in the depth of the awkward silence, the school will start swimming back to you. Nobody likes the silent treatment. Watch a good interviewer on TV. You'll see how they use silence as a strategy, and sometimes as a trap, allowing the negative space to form a hole into which the unwary subject will stumble and fall. A not-so-good interviewer will harangue and declaim and raise their voice above the shouting, with the other party saying 'If you'd just let me finish' and 'Do you mind if I speak?'. The good interviewer just nods, takes mental notes, and waits for just the right opportunity to ask just the right question. Sometimes this tactic is accidental, the by-product of personality rather than strategy. American journalist and author Joan Didion was so painfully shy in her early years as a newspaper reporter that she would clam up during interviews, and her subjects would talk and talk to paper over the silences. That way, she ended up getting great stories.

When it comes to leadership, silence can be a form of power. It can be unnerving to face someone who is just sitting there, saying nothing. We feel vulnerable and judged; our nerves dissolve into words – and they will almost always be the wrong ones. But silence can be a form of strength too. It can stand for compassion, respect, a willingness to *audi alteram partem*: to listen to the other side. Where there is conflict in the air, silence can equally indicate confidence and maturity, an ability to stand your ground and rise above the hubbub. This doesn't apply only to the spoken word. Consider the battle zone of Twitter, where a single ill-considered remark or an unpopular opinion can unleash the fury of the crowd. Sometimes, the best response is no response. Your constitutional right to freedom of expression includes the right to refrain from expressing yourself. Of course, it's a lot less entertaining for your followers, and it negates the very purpose of social media, which is to provide a platform for us to mediate socially. We have voices. We want to speak, and we want to be heard. But the paradox of silence is that the silence speaks for itself.

I stand on the stage now, looking out into the crowd, sweeping my gaze all the way from the front row to the back. My four seconds are up. I break the silence. 'You know, on the way here today, I was thinking—'

The journey has begun, and I can see from the faces that everyone in the room is travelling with me. It's going to be a fun ride. We'll pause along the way, and in good time we'll get to our destination, which is that happy state of knowing something – perhaps many things – that the audience didn't know when the lights went down.

6

The Attitude Adjustment Klap

The black guy in the room;
the Marie Antoinette problem; and
the very persistent illusion of reality

In the early years of my career in business, before I sprouted wings and learnt how to breathe fire, taking on the dragon form of a solo entrepreneur, I worked for a big wholesale cash-and-carry group in Johannesburg, where my immediate superior was a man who wielded his authority like a god. To tell the truth, he was GOD – group operations director, to give him his full, formal title. For the most part, we got along just fine, and he taught me a lot about the hard-and-fast game of fast-moving consumer goods, where the margins are as thin as a scraping of butter on a slice of bread, but the bread is thick enough to keep you in business.

At one stage, I was running a division with an annual turnover of R463 million, which I had grown from R16 million, by supplying foodstuffs and other basic commodities on tender to big government institutions. I was an executive divisional operations director, with a seat on the ops board. My division held the record for the highest compound annual growth rate and EBITDA (earnings before interest, taxes, depreciation and amortisation) in the group. I was 25 years old. But there was something else that set me apart, an aspect of my being that was a source of deep pride, as much as a point of persistent pressure. I was the black guy in a room full of white guys. Until, one day, I wasn't.

I walked into the office one Monday morning, to learn that there had been a bosberaad of executives and directors at the weekend. A bosberaad – that grand old South African tradition of a getaway in the bush, a golden opportunity to spot game, relax in the sun, stand around the braai with beer or brandy in hand, and in between, sit in a conference room and talk about strategy on PowerPoint. An indaba, as we Zulus call it, where the izinDuna, the principal men of the community, gather to mull over important matters, just with less PowerPoint. And to this indaba, I hadn't been invited. I couldn't understand why. I thought I had proved myself; I thought I would have had a few small points to share about organisational strat, about the transformation

The Attitude Adjustment Klap

of vision and mission and values into profit. And maybe even, in the low crackle of a bushveld twilight, about the best type of wood to use on a braai. The crazy thing was, I had been hired by the CEO of the company in the first place, on a gamble, after he heard me speaking to the ExCo at a corporate function. And what had I spoken about? Strategy.

So, after not being invited to the retreat, I went to speak to GOD. His door was always open. I was expecting him to listen, nod, steeple his hands, grant me the grace of his counsel. Instead, we had a raging argument. 'Give me one good reason why I wasn't invited,' I said. He could have told me, as my superior and the convenor of the indaba, and I would have been able to see the glimmer of his point, I suppose – that I was still young and new and inexperienced, and that I could gladly come along to the next bosberaad and give a presentation to the board. But what he actually told me, his now very conspicuously white face turning red with exasperation – he wasn't capable of embarrassment – was something that almost knocked me out, and not in a good way. 'Vusi,' he said, 'we didn't have a place on the jet.'

It was 2010. The year of the FIFA World Cup. Everywhere the flags were flying, from cars, from minibuses, from balconies, from bridges, a blazing canvas of colour and celebration. We were united, one people, one nation, with a goal even greater than the goal Siphiwe Tshabalala scored, to the deafening rasp of the massed vuvuzelas, in the opening match against Mexico at Soccer City. And here I was, left behind on the bench, watching as the jet etched its contrails in the clear blue sky.

To be black, in business, in South Africa, is to drift in perpetual wonder: am I in business only because I'm black? Am I being sidelined only because I'm black? Am I being empowered, am I being disempowered, only because I'm black? I remember one day, at the cash-and-carry business, when the consultants came in to measure the pulse of our blackness. My heart beat faster, louder, when I was told that I was going to be scored as a director, for bonus BEE points. The point is, I wasn't a director; I was an ordinary executive, on a lower pay scale than my fellow execs, who didn't have the necessary qualification – an excess of melanin – to help notch up the points. So I put my big black foot down. I wasn't going to stand up and be counted. GOD called me into his office. 'Vusi,' he said, 'we need you to do this for the team.' Sorry, I said, but no.

I had a heavy burden of responsibility on my shoulders.

The Attitude Adjustment Klap

I was struggling to deliver margins on a big tender where the chain of BEE was being broken by a white supplier, whose input costs I couldn't control. The system, designed to boost black business, was actually making it easy for white business to make a buck behind the scenes. Technically, the practice is called fronting. And here I was, being asked to front myself, to pretend to be something I wasn't. I felt like a sheriff who gets given a badge and is sent onto the streets in a cowboy movie, only to realise, as the bad guys gallop in, that he hasn't been given a gun.

So let me shoot my mouth off about black economic empowerment. It isn't working. That's because, in its most visible form, it isn't working at all: it's about sitting back and amassing wealth, without anyone really having to get their hands dirty. The biggest mistake in the afterglow of democracy in 1994 was the creation of a system of transactions that focused on share ownership, allowing a handful of well-connected individuals to get instant access to companies that had been built up over generations. That's not black economic empowerment. That's black economic enrichment. As a result, you have an economic class that thinks wealth accumulation is easy money. Why would you want to set up a business, and run it for eighteen hours a day, and deal with all the labour issues and supply issues, when you can just gather your shares and run with them?

Recently, I took part in a public debate with someone from the Black Business Council. We need BEE, she said; I said, I completely agree with you, which in the lexicon of debating means 'but wait for the "but"'. The 'but' was, 'But – I'd just like to ask you a question for clarity: how many companies do you run now, exactly?'

'I would prefer us not to personalise this,' she said, and I begged her to indulge me with an answer. I wasn't trying to demean her achievements in any way. I just wanted to quantify. 'Eighteen or so,' she said, after giving it some thought.

'Well, I run two companies, and I don't sleep at night.' So I followed up: 'Within those eighteen companies, how many black people are you personally seeing through an education or schooling programme?'

'I'm not sure,' she said. 'That's the function of HR.'

To me, therein lies the problem. I will call it the Marie Antoinette problem, because it makes me picture the South African economy as a piece of cake, with baked-in layers, strata of living, that keep us apart even a quarter of a century after apartheid. At the base, the foundation, we have the masses of the black working class, whose lives have changed little in the new democracy, and whose prospects for a better life remain bleak, despite the recurring promises of the politicians who seek their votes. Then we have the rising black middle class, many of whom appear to be basking in the glow of the good life – with a cluster home in the suburbs, a shiny SUV, a high-fashion wardrobe – but who in reality are sinking deeper and deeper into debt as they aspire to things beyond their means. Then, above that, we find the black capitalist class, enriched by share ownership schemes and the state tender system. And, on top of it all, the icing on the cake, the small white elite, who still control the bulk of the economy and who enjoy the highest standards of living in the country, according to the Institute of Race Relations Quality of Life Index for 2017 (an index on which white people score 8,1 out of 10, and black people score 5,2).

Where do I fit in here? Which is my slice of the cake? If you were to ask me in public, I would say, I'm one with the people, but come on. I can't remember the last time I slept in a shack, or washed my face with cold water from a zinc tub, or studied by the light of a flickering candle . . . I can't tell you what that feels like now. I mean, look at me, I'm with the bourgeoisie. You might find me on a Sunday morning having breakfast at the Waterford Estate in Stellenbosch, the full English, in the dapple of the vineyards, before heading to Franschhoek – that corner of a foreign field where Marie Antoinette would have felt quite at home – to stroll among the veterans and the vintages at the motor museum in the shadow of the mountain. You can't tell me that black people don't have class, or that they don't feel the need to prove it to each other when they've reached a certain level in the layer cake of status. It is necessary to make a statement, a visible statement, about how far you've travelled, but, counter-intuitively, you have to make an understatement at the same time. So, if you drive a Mercedes S-Class, and Mercedes releases a new S-Class, you don't buy it, because to drive the latest model is to suggest that you have only just arrived. My S-Class is eight years old, which could be taken to mean that I've been on the level for long enough not to have to make a show of it, or that I'm still paying off my car. In ambiguity lies power.

But let us get back to BEE for a moment. I run my own venture capital fund for black entrepreneurs and, every now and again, someone will kick-start the hopes-and-dreams conversation by telling me they are a Level 1 enterprise. That means, of course, that they can tick the little box on the BEE scorecard that says they are 100 per cent black-owned. Wait a second, I always want to say. So you're telling me that your chief business advantage is that you're 100 per cent black? That's when I want to give them what I call an AAK: an attitude adjustment klap. (Don't worry, it's just a figure of speech – my martial-arts training has taught me, above all else, the value of restraint.) But the attitude I want to adjust here is the attitude that if you are a black entrepreneur, you are black first, and an entrepreneur second. In reality, it's the other way round. There are certain laws that govern the way the world works. One of them is the law of gravity, which says that if you jump into the air, no matter how high, you're going to come back down to earth. Another is the law of business. That law says that it takes time to build a business. It's a long, slow process, marked by pain and learning. In building a business, you make mistakes.

If you're lucky, they won't be big as my mistakes, which left me sleeping in my car in the basement of an office park in Centurion, too scared to go back home in case someone came to repossess my car, too scared to go up to the office in case someone knocked on the door to ask for rent. I jumped too high, and I landed with a bang.

But I landed. Some of the entrepreneurs who come to see me, they just want to fly, without ever touching the ground. This young guy came in the other day, looking for half a million rand to grow his business. He's a distributor of moringa, a plant with supposed health benefits. And, on the face of it, he's doing well: he's turning over R12 million a year. But we do the due diligence, and it turns out that he's a million bucks in the red. Why? Well, he says, it's because his stock has been disappearing.

'Where do you keep your stock?' I ask.

'In the garages of my customers.' Well, of course it's been disappearing! What did he think would happen? His customers are taking the stock and selling it and not giving him the money. Since we're talking about plants here, I give him some advice that maybe I shouldn't. I tell him that he needs to start thinking like a Colombian drug lord. Colombian drug lords don't give their customers the goods on a hold-and-buy basis. 'But I was trying to manage costs,' he says. No. You have 72 distribution points around the country, and you have no accounting system, no inventory-management system. You're trying to cut corners.

The Attitude Adjustment Klap

I see this often. I call it the cancer of short-term thinking. I'm not saying it's only a black thing, but it is a black thing. When you live in a system, or you're the product of a system, that boxes you in according to your race, and then boxes you in according to where you live, and boxes you in according to your concept of what you can become, it shouldn't be surprising that you struggle to see the wide-open sky for the walls that surround you. This is the worst thing the system ever did to us. It dumbed down our minds, blinkered our vision, thwarted our aspirations, like a valve that closes a gas cylinder so that it can't be ignited.

How else, case in point, do we explain the curious anomaly of the South African stokvel? This ingenious communal savings and investment vehicle makes up an informal micro-economy that has more than 11 million participants and a total value of some R50 billion. Stokvel, a word meaning 'stock fair', was inspired by the cattle auctions of the nineteenth century, where farmers would gather to socialise and buy livestock. Also, nowadays, known as a gooi-gooi, because you get together with friends, neighbours, family and colleagues to gooi money into a pot, the lump sum of which is then distributed on a rotating basis to members of the collective. The money might be used for groceries, education, home renovations, investing on the JSE, debt repayment, a deposit on a car . . . My dad even belonged to a whisky stokvel, where the cash would be used to buy bottles of Scotland's finest export, to be enjoyed in the finest of company.

As we all know, a stokvel is as good an excuse as any to throw a party. But it's more than that: it's as good an excuse as any to start a bank. There is a small investment stokvel, established in 1995 in the Eastern Cape, that collectively raises R300 000 a year to put into the stock exchange. That's a whole lot of stok, and a whole lot of vel, especially when you multiply it by two and a half decades.

But that's small change compared to, say, Absa, which generates R4,6 billion in turnover a year, using pretty much the same business model: a pool of communal savings, which are then reinvested in the markets.

But why, with all this depth of acumen and activity, with all these stokvels taking place once a month in cities, townships and villages across the nation, with all this capital flowing into and out of the pot, is there still not one single successful black-owned bank in South Africa? I'll tell you why. It's because we think small. It's because we can't see beyond the walls. It's because we all need an attitude adjustment klap.

The Attitude Adjustment Klap

Have you ever wondered why there is no nation on earth where Jewish people, en masse, are poor? Why, despite generations of persecution and suffering, the Jewish people have not only survived, but prospered and thrived? I have wondered too, and I think it comes down to a way of thinking, a way of taking responsibility for one's own destiny and, then, of putting that to work. There is a word that sums this up, a word you will hear often in the boardrooms, the lecture rooms, the conference rooms, the bosberaads: 'agency'. We all have agency. It means the power to seize power for ourselves, to take charge, to take ownership. If I accept that I have agency, it means that I accept the trajectory of my life, and that I am ultimately in charge of it. If, on the other hand, I choose to disassociate myself from this power and agency, it means I can turn around and say, this is how my life has turned out – it is because of the system, because of apartheid, because of white monopoly capital. It's never because of me.

You know who appreciates this message? That's right: white people. Every time I talk about agency, white people say, thank you, thank you, because white people can't say it; they would be seen to be racist. But when I say it to a black person, when I say, you've got to take charge, you've got to take ownership, you've got to take responsibility for the successes and failures of your life, they will almost always say: that's easy for you to say, because you're Vusi.

But, hey, I've had my attitude adjustment klaps too. Mostly from my mother, who was never a student of the martial arts, and who therefore never had to worry about restraint. She could just klap. But she didn't. She was the therapist in the home, especially after my father died. She taught us self-confidence and self-esteem and believing in ourselves, even when we didn't have the means. I remember the day of the big public-speaking championships. I was seventeen. It was the finals. I was up against Adam, from Crawford High, a phenomenal speaker, and a young lady from Parktown, Kate, whom I used to call Kiss Me Kate, because she never would. I was winning, marginally, on the prepared speeches, but I was dreading the impromptu, because that part was my weak point. You need to be a reader to be good at impromptu, because when you read, you're creating all the time, you're actively producing pictures in your mind. But I was a movie watcher. And when you watch movies, you're just consuming. You're not thinking or visualising for yourself.

The Attitude Adjustment Klap

So I'm standing outside, during the break, on this beautiful lawn of an office park in Sandton, and I'm shit-nervous. I'm taking deep breaths, trying to stop the trembling. My mom comes over. She looks at me – she can see I'm in a state – and she says, 'Vusi, I just want to tell you that I'm proud of you.' Sure, Mom, I'm thinking. Thanks. I've heard you tell me this before. But she carries on: 'I'm proud of you not because of how far you've come. That you've come this far is not an achievement. You've always been capable of that.' She looks me in the eye now. 'I'm proud of you,' she says, almost whispering, 'because I know you're going to go up there and win this competition.'

My topic for the impromptu was 'Reality is an illusion, albeit a very persistent one'. I think Einstein said it. We were all given ten minutes to prepare, and then, one by one, we moved into the room.

Adam spoke about how reality TV is in reality an illusion. A brilliant and illuminating speech. Kate spoke about the point at which we all live our lives, at the intersection between reality and illusion. A brilliant and mind-opening speech. Then it was my turn. I spoke about growing up as a young black man, about the shadow that history cast over me, about the legacy of the Land Act, the Immorality Act, the Group Areas Act, that confined my parents and my grandparents to boxes within boxes, and I spoke about the reality of the new society, with its promise of democracy and freedom and a better life for all, and how that reality had turned out to be an illusion, albeit a very persistent one.

My mom was right: I won the competition. I could feel the walls shattering all around me. And today, when I look to the skies, I think to myself, I'm in charge, I can own this, I may not be able to defy gravity, but I can fly. And the next time a jet plane soars up there, into the wide, blue open, it's not going to leave me behind.

7

There is No B in 'Team'

Hustle, muscle, folly and smarts;
a Tinder for jobs; why we have to fight against
the 'ag-shame!' narrative

Every entrepreneur, every 'wantrepreneur', every dreamer who ever dared to venture into the Dragons' Den, will have in mind a model of their better self, a vision of the hero they would most like to be. For some, it will be Steve Jobs, the tempestuous revolutionary who built the most successful technology company in the world. For some, it will be Oprah Winfrey, the talk-show humanitarian who rose up from poverty to found an empire of entertainment with a purpose. For others, it will be Elon Musk, the sci-fi nerd whose childhood fantasies blazed a trail for self-driving cars and voyages to the stars.

As for me, well, I don't have a single role model of entrepreneurial aptitude and endeavour. No; instead, I have four.

One is a guy by the name of Bosco 'BA' Baracus. The 'BA' stands for 'bad attitude' – a testament to his chronic inability to suffer fools gladly. He is big, black, beefy, bare-chested, bedecked with chains of gold. He wears a Mohawk cut and has a scowl permanently welded onto his face.

Then there is John 'Hannibal' Smith, an urbane, cigar-smoking master of disguise, who sees life as an easy-going adventure, and whose battle-planning prowess is a tribute to the legendary Carthaginian general from whom he takes his nickname.

Next in the crew is Templeton 'Faceman' Peck, a smooth-talking, sharp-dressed hustler, who can wangle his way into or out of any face-to-face situation. And finally, we have HM 'Howling Mad' Murdock, a wide-eyed, certifiably crazy wingman, who wears a battered leather flight jacket, khaki fatigues, a baseball cap and basketball sneakers, and who can fly any type of aircraft with fearless skill and precision.

Together – and, as Hannibal is fond of saying, I love it when a plan comes together – they make up one of the greatest problem-solving, fugitive-on-the-run commando squads in history: the A-Team. I grew up watching their exploits on television, enthralled not just by the gun-toting, face-punching, blowing-things-up action, but by the way the foursome managed to overcome their differences. BA was always telling Murdock to 'shut up, fool', to get the job done. Their secret, I now realise, was that they weren't just the A-Team; they were a team, born in creative conflict, brought together by circumstance, their individual talents and energies fused in a coalition that was greater than the sum of its parts. Of course, it helped that they were totally imaginary too, the product of a Hollywood TV studio, which meant they could get out of any difficulty with a retake or a catchphrase or a special effect. But, even in the real world, the world of seething freeway traffic, interminable Power-Point presentations, high call-centre call volumes, and plans that fall apart, there is much we can learn from these indefatigable alpha males.

The A-Team are my entrepreneurial role models because here's what it takes to be an entrepreneur: the brute strength of Baracus; the strategic acumen of Hannibal; the confident salesmanship of Faceman; and perhaps above all else, the howling madness of Howling Mad Murdock. To leave the comfort and security of a well-paid job, like I did, and start a new enterprise afresh calls for that same mix of hustle, muscle, folly and smarts. But it calls, also, for other people, people who can share the journey to the distant shore, and in the process challenge and complement and bring out the best in us. We do not sail this ship – the entrepreneur ship – alone.

Is there such a thing, I wonder, as a Tinder for jobs? I would swipe left, left, left, left, left . . . until I found somebody who looked right for the job. If only it were that simple. At Google, there is a mantra that is used in the Department of People Operations (they're Google, they would never just call it HR): 'Watch the door, watch the door, watch the door.' It means, take a look at the quality, aptitude, and 'fit' of people from the moment they walk in; hire right, right from the start. Google gets about 2 million job applications a year, of which about 5 000 get the nod. That makes the company about 25 times more selective than Harvard or Yale. Former senior vice president of people operations at Google, Laszlo Bock, once told an interviewer that a hopeful applicant had sent him a sneaker by post, hoping that this 'foot in the door' would land him a job. It's not that easy.

It's a sad reality that we have an unemployment rate of 48 per cent among black South Africans aged between 18 and 35, my prime young talent pool, and a lot of young hopefuls will be taking a chance on any prospect they can get. They'll be sitting in an internet cafe, firing off emails for call-centre jobs, admin jobs, operations jobs, in the hope that sooner or later one of them will hit the target. I'm not the CEO of Absa. I'm a niche player in a niche market that is moving very fast, growing more and more competitive by the day. I don't have the luxury of being a nice guy, of taking in starry-eyed hopefuls and mentoring, guiding, and up-training them until, one day, they reach the stars. With me, it's the opposite: I need to find proven A-players who can get right down to business and help me grow.

Running a small company, as I do, an investment and advisory consultancy, means that I look for people who can manage by themselves, who can lace up their sneakers and fleet-foot it to the finish on any task or project, no matter how big or small. It means that I look for the A-players: the strong, the smart, the persuasive, the slightly – just a little, and this is a fine line – crazy in the head. It's a tough proposition, putting together an A-team, because A-players don't always present as A-players. As WB Yeats reminds us, in those famous lines from 'The Second Coming', 'The best lack all conviction, while the worst are full of passionate intensity.' So you can't hire on passionate intensity alone; you need to look for the deeper, more subtle qualities, that will most likely only reveal themselves in full much further down the line – the qualities of vulnerability, of humility, of an innate ability to reflect, self-criticise, and correct.

And you look too for someone who, if they are walking through the lobby and they see a client waiting there, will not just ask if they would like a cup of tea, but will go and make it too. 'It's not my job.' I feel so strongly about these words that I consider the uttering of them in my company to be a dismissible offence. Make the tea. And while you're about it, go ahead and make a cup for yourself. You've earned it.

But what else do A-team players do? It is tempting to say, simply, that they do their best at everything they do, but you could just as easily say that about B-players. That's how Avis built its brand in the car-rental business, by forever trying harder to beat the A-players at their own game. 'Best' is a fleeting standard, one that you set in order to surpass it, and to illuminate the trail for others to follow.

For an A-player, ever-restless, ever-questing, the next thing they do will always be the best thing they do. Which reminds me of a story about Steve Jobs, except it is really a story about someone who worked with Steve Jobs. In 1985, after a tumultuous power struggle, which led to Jobs storming out of Apple, the company he had founded, he founded another computer company, called NeXT. As the name suggests, Jobs wanted to take the concept of the personal computer to the next level, what he called the interpersonal computer, capable of connecting with other computers to form a multimedia communications network that would change the way people worked. We're used to that now – we call it the internet – but back then it was a radical, game-changing notion. Jobs wanted a corporate logo that would reflect that, and be just as memorable in the public mind as the apple with the bite taken out of it. So he hired a designer, the best designer in the world at the time, a man whose portfolio included the logos of UPS, Westinghouse and, most famously, IBM, with its monumental horizontally striped letters instantly evoking the dynamic pace of change in the computer era. His name was Paul Rand. He was an A-player, and so was Steve Jobs. The best in the business was hiring the best in the business. It was inevitable that there would be a butting of heads, a clash of egos and temperaments and artistic visions.

Jobs, with his hands-on style of micro-management and his deep-rooted design sensibility, said he wanted to see a range of options for the logo, a not unusual request in any creative brief. But, according to Walter Isaacson's biography of Jobs, this is how the designer, crotchety and in his 70s, responded: 'I will solve your problem, and you will pay me. You can use what I produce, or not, but I will not do options, and either way you will pay me.' The fee was $100 000 – a fortune for the time. Jobs backed down, and two weeks later he got his logo, a skewed black cube containing the letters NeXT in four bright colours. The company may have disappeared, but the logo remains as one of the most eye-catching designs of the modern age.

No options. Here we have a case study in the way A-players think and work. They don't bring their B-game to the table, because they don't have a B-game, a backup, a just-in-case. A-players are single-minded, focused and driven, and there is no ceiling to their capability and ambition. Take Michelangelo, who was commissioned by the reigning Pope to do that paint job on the Sistine Chapel in Rome. The Pope wanted just the twelve apostles, but Michelangelo had loftier plans, and he was finally given the go-ahead to do as he pleased, which is why the ceiling today consists of 33 panels displaying more than 300 figures, covering all the bases from the Creation to the Last Judgement. The Pope wasn't given options.

It's important to remember when you hire an A-player for your own team that you are not hiring a set of excuses or apologies or options. You are hiring a set of solutions to your problems. I may not be Steve Jobs or the Pope, but I too am always looking for someone who can do the job, fix the problem, tackle the toughest task, and if they have to go over my head to do it, fine, I'll just sit back and enjoy the view.

But the trouble with A-players is that they're hard to find. As part of my recruitment process, in the first round of interviews, I always give the candidate an assignment to do, to test their ability to see if they will fit into the role. They have 48 hours to do the assignment and deliver. And more than once – and this has been the case with candidates who were otherwise very promising – I've heard the excuse: 'Oh, but I don't have a computer.' Wait, so how did you manage to email me your application for the job? How are you going to be able to solve my problems, when you can't figure out a way to solve your own?

At the other end of the scale, there was this young lady who went out and wrote her entire assignment by hand, having done all her research on her cellphone, and hopped into a taxi to deliver her assignment to me on time. She didn't get the job, but boy, was I impressed! 'A' for 'attitude', all the way. Strictly speaking, that's not one of the criteria I use when hiring. The process is a bit more scientific than that. I've been caught flat-footed too often when I've gone with my gut in deciding whether or not a person is an A-player. So now I use science: a strict method of calculation, based on five categories of assessment, each given a score out of ten. If you don't score eight or above in each category, then sorry, but you're not an A-player.

Let's start with presentation, the 'watch the door' part, as they say at Google. How do you walk, how do you talk, how do you generally carry and present yourself? I'm not going to ask you to sing – this isn't *Idols*, but first impressions do count, and if you dress for an interview with a financial consultancy firm as if you're dressing for a night out at the club (I actually once had a candidate who was dressed like that), it means you haven't read or understood the job spec.

Then there is what I call 'fit to culture'. Yes, I'm afraid so. That vague, contentious concept that nobody quite understands when it is applied to a corporation, as opposed to a nation, clan or tribe. Culture, in the corporate sense, is typically taken to mean the values, beliefs and attitudes of the collective workforce, and how they are moulded from the inside in a way that can be projected to the outside.

We all have a sense, partly through our exposure to marketing and branding, partly through our direct experience of services and products, of the distinct individual cultures of, say, Google, Apple, Nando's, BMW, Coca-Cola and Amazon. But I prefer to see culture as a far more practical force, defined and given meaning by the work a company does to justify its reason for being. Culture is work; work is culture, and the way you approach and produce your work will determine whether or not you fit the culture.

In my company, I split the culture fit into three components. The first component is eight o'clock to five o'clock thinking, which we don't do. That is a relic of the Industrial Age, when workers would clock in and out of the workplace for an allotted portion of the day, outside of which they would mysteriously no longer be workers. We see a hangover of this in the out-of-office email reply, which fools nobody and should be outlawed. I mean, come on. Your smartphone is your office, and you are never, ever out of it. Everyone knows you are flicking through your mail, in between watching Netflix or lounging on the beach. (All right, I admit, I speak for myself here.) But the rules of work have changed, and one of them is that we no longer work to rule.

The second cultural subclause here, as previously discussed, is that nobody in the company says, 'It's not my job.' Your job description is your job description, plus anything else you are asked to do, with one proviso: you shouldn't have to be asked to do it. It should come naturally. In the new culture of the workplace, renaissance thinking will be your greatest asset. Many years ago, there was a man who applied for a job, and in his curriculum vitae he listed a long string of capabilities that included the following: building bridges, emptying trenches, destroying fortresses, unleashing mortars, designing and arming sea-going vessels, manufacturing indestructible chariots and constructing secret pathways under rivers. With every listing, he was presenting himself primarily as a solver of problems – an A-player. And then, right at the foot of his CV, almost as an afterthought, he added: 'I can carry out sculpture in marble, bronze, or clay, and also I can do in painting whatever may be done.' The man's name was Leonardo da Vinci, and he was applying for a position, any position, with the Duke of Milan. He got the job. Be like Leonardo. Be unafraid to try anything. You'll go far.

Finally, under fit to culture, and this may seem counter-intuitive in light of the foregoing, we have this mantra: 'Family first'. I expect anyone who works with me to find the time to be with their family, and to relish and cherish those moments. I know I do.

The next two categories of assessment are industry knowledge and company knowledge. I used to be impressed when interviewing people to hear them telling me what they knew about me and my business, but, to be honest, that doesn't turn me on any more. I now realise and recognise that all it indicates is a passing familiarity with the tools of the World Wide Web. Now I look for something deeper than gleanings of information: I look for jewels of insight. I run a financial services firm. What are my greatest challenges? What are my greatest opportunities? Who are my chief competitors? What are their strategies? What are their strengths and weaknesses? What can we and should we be doing better, to beat them? Go ahead. I'm listening . . .

And then there is the category I call 'history to role fit'. What this means is, have you historically performed a role where there was a fit of duties, however slight, with the duties you would be performing here? If you had previously worked as a receptionist, say, and you were applying for a job in sales, I wouldn't hire you, unless – and this is something I've actually done – you had also worked as a distributor of Herbalife at the weekend. You've sold, in other words. And because of that, I'm sold.

So those are the five categories, with a total possible score of 50 points. If you score 40 or above, you're an A-player and, as they say on *Idols*, congratulations, you're through to the next round! Care to apply?

But I'm not just talking about my game here. I'm talking about any game you may be in, and why you should strive to play it to the level of 'A', because who wants to be seen as anything less than that? It pains me to see how often we take less than as the standard. Why is it okay for us to just be okay, why do we allow ourselves to fall victim to the 'ag, shame' narrative? 'Ag, shame! He's just a young black guy. Give him a chance, he's trying his best.' If we accept that, we will never succeed. We must be the ones who hold each other accountable, who raise our expectations high enough for others to raise themselves higher. We must be the ones saying, 'No, excuse me, I don't accept this level of service from your spaza shop.' From your garage. From your call centre. From your multibillion-rand commercial bank.

Anyone can be an A-player, a problem-solver, a difference-maker. You know those guys you see at the airport, when you rush in to use the bathroom before you board your flight, and they stand there giving you a bright smile and a warm greeting – 'Welcome to my office!' – and the sign on the wall says 'Toilet Manager'. They're bringing their A-game. You can too. Be strong. Be confident. Be resourceful. Be bold, creative, a little bit crazy. Who knows? Maybe one day, when your plan comes together, you'll get a call from the A-Team too.

8
A Kota Loaf is Better than None

Sweetening a business deal;
turning a snack into a franchise; and
the big trouble with thinking small

It was the day of my uncle's funeral. On waves of song, we sent him to his rest in the red soil, from where his spirit would rise to watch over us in eternal memory. On the other side of the great divide, we, the living, moved on with our duties and preoccupations, one of which was lunch.

As I sat with my plate piled high, chatting quietly with friends and family, a delegation of four young boys approached the table. I thought they had come to offer their commiserations, but from their shy giggles and the way they were nudging each other, I could tell they had something else in mind. They greeted me politely, and then stood for a moment, as if to gather their thoughts and pluck up their courage. Finally, one of them spoke, and I realised, even in the midst of this strictly social occasion, that they wanted to talk business. Serious business. 'Please,' said the little tyke, with the plaintive air of Oliver Twist asking for seconds, 'we are looking for five rand.' Aha! That's what you get for being a dragon, I thought.

In 2014, on the Mzansi channel on M-Net, I was one of five such creatures, chosen to sit on the jury of the South African edition of a reality TV series called *Dragons' Den*. One tends to think of a dragon as a fearsome beast, part reptile, part bird of prey, swooping from the stormy skies, breathing fire and demanding ritual sacrifices from the petrified populace. Then comes St George, charging in on his noble steed, to lance the dragon and rescue the princess from its daggerlike claws. In the modern lore of business, the saintly entrepreneur will set out to do much the same thing, striding forth to challenge the new day with a mixture of bravado and righteous zeal. True, the weapon will be pen on paper, rather than lance on horseback, but the point will remain: to slay the dragon.

As for *Dragons' Den*, I and my fellow panellists – media mogul Lebo Gunguluza, investment banker and start-up funder Polo Leteka Radebe, ad agency owner Gil Oved and serial tech entrepreneur Vinny Lingham – were the dragons.

A Kota Loaf is Better than None

As we sat in our tribunal, a procession of inventors, tinkerers and idea-mongers would parade their wares and business plans in a bid to persuade us to invest a specified amount in exchange for a stake in the enterprise.

Naturally, we were not that easy to convince, especially because – and this is the kicker that gives the series its appeal – it was our own money that was on the line. We were angels who feared to tread, weighing up the risks with great care, while holding on to our foolish belief that maybe, just maybe, the next bright idea would be the one to change the world.

So, here I was at the funeral, Vusi the Dragon, being asked to pony up five bucks in venture capital by a bunch of kids who offered no collateral or start-up proposal whatsoever. I was going to have to teach them a lesson. I reached into my pocket, pulled out a R5 coin and told them they could have it – with a term and condition attached. They were going to have to raise an equal amount from at least one other adult at the funeral. Off they ran, rushing from table to table, this time with no evident trepidation. A few minutes later, they returned, gleefully brandishing their treasure. My word was my deed. I handed over the coin. Now they had a whole ten bucks in their war chest. What were they planning to do with it? Save it for a rainy day? Split it four ways? Invest it in a spread of equities on the JSE? 'We're going to buy sweets!' they answered, as one. Sweet. But I wasn't done with them yet.

Money is a fleeting gift. If you spend it, it's as if you never had it. If you keep it, it's as if you'll never need it. But if you trade it, if you buy something to sell something, then you're on your way to unlocking the secret of what money really means, and why it makes the world spin on its axis. You're unlocking the secret of value. I had a good talk with the boys. I told them to buy some sweets from the spaza shop, keep a few for themselves, and see if they could sell the rest to their friends who were playing in the park. We agreed on a price per unit. We settled on the margin spread. 'Remember, boys,' I told them, a flinty edge to my voice. 'Always be closing. Now get out there and sell, sell, sell!'

They came back about an hour later – I suspect they may have been gambling some time on the swings and roundabouts – and showed me their haul. I couldn't believe it either. R25! Even if they returned the seed money to the grown-ups, they would still have been R15 in the black. I hope one day, when they open their nationwide sweet-shop franchise operation, they remember to give some credit to the old guy who sent them on their way. 'That Vusi, what a guy. He taught us everything we know!'

Later that day, as I drove through the township, I was struck once again by the abundance of busy-ness, the number of small and micro-enterprises flourishing there, calling out to customers from storefronts and homefronts and repurposed freight containers. The aircon regassers, the airtime resellers, the boerewors caravans, the hair salons, the car washes, the internet cafes, the tattoo parlours, the computer repairers, the hubcap hawkers, the cobblers, the brickmakers, the dressmakers, the ginger-beer makers. The lively economy of the *lokasie* is a testament to the fortitude and initiative of people working their way up from the edge of poverty, scrabbling a living in the quest to lead a better life. Everywhere you look, you see the small businesses, and every time I see them, I think to myself, okay, so where are the big ones? Yes, it is heartening to see survivalism in action, to know that people are making enough, little by little, day by day, to get by. The trouble with enough, though, is that it is never enough. Still, when it comes to our daily bread, half a loaf, as we say, is better than none. But why settle for half a loaf, when you could treat yourself to a nice, hearty kota?

You know the kota, right? You take a quarter loaf of fresh, white, crusty bread – 'government bread', as we call it – you scoop out the guts and refill it to the brim with sausages, chicken, polony, ham, cheese, fried eggs, burger patties, spicy mince, lamb curry, chilli sauce, atchar, some peri-peri to taste. You cram some vegetables in there too, because everyone knows vegetables are good for you. Oh, and the chips. I almost forgot the chips. You stick them in like the struts of a building, you grab the kota with both hands, you squeeze down a little, open your mouth as wide as you can, and you eat. The kota is the signature street cuisine of the kasi, our answer to the dainty triangular sandwiches that the colonialists brought to our shores. No thank you. The joy of a kota is that it is filling twice over: first you fill the belly of the bread, then you fill your own.

But as much as I enjoy a good kota, it has become for me a symbol of everything that is wrong with the way we think about and do business at the breadline of our economy. I see it as symptomatic of a failure of vision, of imagination, of big-picture planning, of opportunity slipping through our fingers in the way that the atchar does when you bite down on your takeaway. You would think, with so many kotas being eaten by so many people in so many corners of the country, that there would be a ready niche for a big kota business. And you would be right.

I met a guy by the name of Tibo who runs a kota outlet in Alexandra, across the freeway from Sandton. He set it up, small-scale, in 2005, and within ten years he had created three additional jobs and was turning over more than R50 000 a year. Now head onto London Road from Alex, and drive east for about twenty minutes, until you get to the central business district of Edenvale. Here you will find no Valley of Eden, but you will find, between the sentinels of the towering palms, an establishment called Kota Joe, a roadhouse in the grand American tradition, with a giant illuminated menu running across the wall, and a slogan that advises you to save your discretion for another day. 'Screw the Diet', it proclaims, and the menu is the reason why, with a selection of kotas stuffed into Portuguese rolls, and luminous double-thick milkshakes sludged into one-litre containers. Kota Joe was not founded by some township guy named Joe; it was founded by Paul Figueira, an entrepreneur who saw a gap in the townships, started selling kotas in brightly branded freight containers, and then got a capital injection that allowed him to launch a fast-growing franchise business that was turning over more than R20 million in its first three years.

What is the big difference between Tibo in Alex and Paul all-over-the-place? Is it just the colour of their skin? Is it privilege versus oppression? Is it easy access to networks and funding, versus the lingering legacy of a social and political system that sought to reduce the majority of the population to drawers of water and hewers of wood? I think it cuts even deeper than that. It cuts across centuries and generations, across the great divide of culture and class. It cuts into the heart and mind. In the township where I grew up, there was a railway line fringed by patches of veld, and on the other side of the line lay a township called Actonville, which was designated according to the Group Areas Act for Asians only. On our side, the homes were small and humble; on the other, they were grand, double-storeyed, almost baronial. On our side, we had little spaza shops selling bread loaves by the fraction, and 'loose draws' – the term for single cigarettes. On the other side, there were rows and rows of family-owned businesses that outgrew their premises and constraints: the dry-cleaner that became a sporting-goods store, the tailor that became a gentlemen's outfitters, the samoosa shop that became a catering empire. The businesses would be handed down from generation to generation, and each new generation would revitalise the business and lead it in a new direction, while honouring the principles on which it was founded. Legacy businesses, as we call them. In the townships, what is our legacy? Our legacy is that we get out of the townships as quickly as we can.

We must be the only people who measure our success not by how many other successes we create, but by how many failures we leave behind. We make money, we move out, we buy fancy cars. And then, on a Saturday, we drive in our fancy cars to the kasi, and we sit at the Shisa Nyama with our friends who couldn't make it out. We'll tell ourselves we're getting back in touch with our roots, as we tuck into our buy-and-braai, and we shift our accent, consciously, from Sandton to township. But what are we really doing? We're affirming ourselves; we're validating our life choices; we're reminding ourselves of the long, hard road we've travelled. But until we create a mindset where we go back to plant new roots, to share the wealth of our knowledge and the equity of our experience, to grow and inspire and uplift, we will not be able to build a better South Africa. Mindset isn't attitude. Mindset is philosophy. Philosophy is what makes

Apple a symbol of the joy of technology, Google a symbol of the power of information, BMW a symbol of the exuberance of driving. Philosophy is the real reason why an entrepreneur can take something as simple and as basic as a kota, and see in it the beginnings of a nationwide fast-food phenomenon. It's the reason why Mr Price, the cut-price retailer, has been able to build a business with an annual turnover of R20 billion, while township fashion entrepreneurs struggle to get their hip designs on the shelves. The trouble with us is, we dream too small.

My dad was a salesman. The best in the business. He would drive all the way from Wattville to Venda and Thabazimbi, and come back with his boot loaded with the best fresh vegetables money could buy. Then he would sell them door to door. It was as easy as selling candy in a crèche. At the end of the day, he would show us his fistful of cash, and we would go out for supper to celebrate. We had money. We were rich! Except, it wasn't our money. It belonged to the business. The next day, the bulk of the takings would be ploughed back into buying fresh stock, and my dad would be back on the road again – and again and again. We were survivalists. We had food on the table. Fresh vegetables, even. For my dad, that was enough; he didn't want to own the farm. Me, I've always been big on the dreams. I don't want to fly business class; I want to own the airline. I don't want to go on holiday; I want to own the island. I don't want to drive a Porsche; I want to own the factory. I don't want to be a survivalist; I want to be a thrivalist. The biggest lie that was ever sold to black people was the lie that they must be satisfied with thinking small. Small business, small prospects, small profits. Big lie!

But the thing about big thinking is that it's not enough – you have to think deep as well. Let me tell you a story about the president. No, not that president – I'm talking about a guy who dared to venture into the Dragons' Den one day, to pitch a business idea and interest us in his invention. His name was Zithande but, as he stood there, in his shiny, grey suit, rocking on his shiny, black heels, his hands clasped in front of him, like a groom at the altar, he looked at us and said, 'You can call me Mr President.' Big thinker. Then he delivered his presidential address. He had come up with a very powerful product that was going to change the world, he assured us. It sat there on an office chair, draped with a black cloth that I knew was going to be whipped off with a flourish at some point. But, first, he ran the numbers by us. He was looking for an investment of R1 million, which he would turn into $100 million in a matter of months. He already had a deal to supply a nationwide chain, with 140 outlets, and there had been interest from the US too. Very big thinker and, in the best entrepreneurial tradition, maybe a little crazy too. Then came the bottom line. He whipped away the cloth to reveal ... a roll of toilet paper, attached by a holder to an upright board. He turned the board around, and on its back side was a push-button liquid dispenser, of the kind you find in the better, smarter public toilets. That was his invention. He called it the iWipe. (Yet another start-up entrepreneur inspired by Steve Jobs, I thought.)

Zithande, or should I say Mr President, explained the workings of his invention to us as we leaned forward in curiosity. You take a handful of toilet paper, you apply water from the dispenser to make it soft and wet, and then, well, you 'iWipe'. Happily, the inventor chose not to demonstrate the use of his invention, but when it came to the moment of passing judgement, all five of us on the panel, sadly, gave it a thumbs down.

Feedback is important for a start-up entrepreneur. Even on reality TV, in the realm of 'you're fired' and 'you are the weakest link', there is nothing more brutal or demoralising than a flat-out no. So, before I gave my verdict, I conceded the merits of the pitch: soft and wet, in the circumstances, was always going to be better than hard and dry. 'Except,' I added, 'there is something called wet wipes. And you can get them at any branch of Dis-Chem.'

The trouble with Mr President was that he had created a solution for a problem that didn't exist. He was spot on about the potential of the market: a report by the market-research company TechNavio predicts that the global value of the 'toilet care' sector will reach more than $6 billion by the end of 2019. But either he hadn't done his own research, or he'd taken a look at a wet wipe one day, had a eureka moment in reverse, deconstructed it to its basic constituents of tissue and H_2O, and thought, let me go and see if I can get a million bucks out of those dragons. He thought big, but not deep.

But then a certain Charmagne came to see us dragons. She was looking for money to start a beauty salon. Hmmm... A crowded market, I thought – how do you even begin to compete against the ubiquitous Sorbet franchise? But she had a vehicle to match her driving ambition. In the lexicon of modern entrepreneurship, she was an 'Uberfor'. As in, an Uber for gardening, an Uber for dog walking, an Uber for household cleaning and maintenance. Such services, which set out to satisfy the deep-rooted human need to conserve as much energy as possible – on the premise that laziness, not necessity, is the true mother of invention – are also known as ODMSes, or on-demand mobile services. You tap an app to summon the service, at your leisure, rather than having to go all the way out to find it.

Charmagne's Uberfor was an Uber for hair styling and beauty, which she called a 360 mobile salon. 'By leveraging innovation and technology, and mobilising our technicians, we offer a unique quality service that is different from the norm,' she told us. By that, she meant she would send her mobile salon out to your home, your office, or the venue for your big event, where you would be beautified and coiffeured for a minimum fee of R800.

Initially, there was some scepticism among the dragons, who questioned whether there were enough customers out there prepared to pay that much for a consultation. But she had come armed with facts and research to back her proposition. Notably, as she told us, some 40 per cent of spend in the beauty and styling business goes on products and peripherals, which makes every consultation an opportunity to up-sell. The more you can make your customers look good, the better things look for your business.

A Kota Loaf is Better than None

We were sold. One by one, we said, 'I'm in' – a pledge that proved to be worth R800 000 in phased-in funding for Charmagne's mobile beauty start-up. Off she went, delighted, to test her service in the market. It was a hit. She had rave reviews from customers on the social-media channels and she was profiled as a role model for young black entrepreneurship by business and lifestyle magazines. Then, something happened to Charmagne's business – something that happens to almost 70 per cent of small businesses in South Africa. It failed.

There is a certain romance attached to the notion of failure as a rite of passage for entrepreneurs, but as a graduate of that school, I can assure you there is nothing romantic about it. Failure in business is brutal and debilitating, and it makes you question everything, including the faith you thought you had in yourself. Sometimes the answer, the one you don't want to hear, is well tried: you've learnt from the experience, now find something else to do with your life. Which is more or less what the majority of the panel, three out of five of us, told Charmagne when she stepped back into the Dragons' Den. She listened, she nodded . . . and she ignored our advice. Well, the advice given by three out of five of us. She sold her flat and moved back into her parents' home. She sold her car and used the proceeds to fund her business for another few months. The last I heard, she was cash-positive, but a long way from being profitable, and a long way from giving me a return on my investment. But you know why I think she'll do well? Because she doesn't think small.

Her market isn't Alex, it isn't Joburg, it isn't Gauteng. Her market is New York, Paris, London, Rome – anywhere you'll find people with a smartphone in their hand and an urgent need to call someone over to make them look good. An Uber for beauty, an Uber for confidence, an Uber for self-esteem. How can that not be the big idea that builds a big business, somewhere down the line? To me, it sounds as easy as giving a pack of kids five bucks to buy some sweets to sell. And I'm pretty sure that one day, no matter how long it takes, I'm going to get my money back from them as well.

9

The Emperor Needs New Clothes

The barbarians at the gate;
how BlackBerry lost the plot; and
the difference between a frog and a butterfly

'Mxm.' It's not a word; it's an attitude. A pop-click of personal percussion, a spark of the tongue against the roof of the mouth. It means, 'I'm done. I've had enough. That's it, end of conversation.' Used this way on social media, especially Twitter, 'mxm' is a rhetorical device that renders all foregoing argument irrelevant. It's like knocking your king over on the chessboard. You concede the game, but it's game over, so it feels like a win when there's no other way out. On Twitter, of course, you are encouraged to condense your thoughts, so it is possible to get by with a very limited lexicon of responses. A 'tjo' when you are shocked or surprised; a 'shem' when you are touched by someone's plight; a 'haibo' when you are shaking your head in disbelief; a 'kwaaa' when you are amused; a 'tltlt' when you are just a little amused; a 'nxa' when you are feeling contented.

But there is nothing in the spoken world beyond the social networks that is more eloquent or forceful than a well-delivered 'mxm', especially when it is accompanied by a sharp upward tilt of the head, to reinforce your righteous indignation.

'Mxm' is what you say when you finally get to the front of the queue at Home Affairs, only to be told that the system is down and you must come back tomorrow. 'Mxm' is what you say when you ease onto the freeway and accelerate, only to see the sun glinting on the long line of static vehicles stretching into the distance. And 'mxm' is what I find myself saying as I watch the baggage carousel going round and round and round, until there is nothing left on it, and I realise that my suitcase has gone to a different destination while I am standing in the airport in Rome. What am I supposed to? I do as the Romans do. I raise my voice, gesture with my hands, and eventually, abandoning all hope, shrug my shoulders and carry on with my own 'la dolce vita'.

The next day, I stand on the stage, wearing jeans, a casual shirt and sneakers. It takes me back to the early days

The Emperor Needs New Clothes

of my career as a public speaker, when I would wear a smart suit with a pair of All Stars – the suit to remind me of how far I had travelled, the All Stars to remind me of where I had begun.

And here I am now, all these years later, in the epicentre of an ancient civilisation, at the heart of what was once a mighty empire that spanned more than 30 countries, covered almost 6 million square kilometres of territory, and was home to some 90 million people, and I look like, or at least I feel like, a barbarian. A stranger, an outsider, a non-belonger, conspicuously un-suited for the occasion and the challenge, which is, oddly enough, to warn people about the invading forces, the pillaging hordes who even now are rattling the gates outside the fortified city walls.

That's right: the barbarians. We're everywhere. But before I issue my warnings, let me quickly define my terms. To call someone a barbarian, in modern society, is to defame them as brutish, coarse and uncouth, unless perhaps you are referring to a member of Barbarian FC, fondly known as the Baa-Baas, the invitation-only British rugby club whose motto is 'Rugby Football is a game for gentlemen in all classes, but for no bad sportsman in any class.' These Barbarians, recruited from the top ranks of national teams around the world, are spirited amateurs who play a few times a year for the sheer love and camaraderie of the game, without, as their creed decrees, the pressure of having to win.

The same cannot be said for their historical namesakes. In its original meaning, a barbarian was simply anyone who did not belong to your culture or speak your language, which is why the Ancient Greeks dubbed them *bárbaros*, or 'babblers'. By that definition, there are a lot of us babblers around, just as there were in the days when the Roman Empire was at the peak of its influence and power. The barbarian tribes, whose names will be familiar to students of history and Asterix – among them the Gauls, the Goths, the Celts, the Saxons and the Iberians – were scattered, restless and diverse, and the empire kept them in check by granting them land in exchange for their loyalty. Then the trouble began. The barbarians wanted more land; they wanted a share of the immense wealth, luxury and privilege that the Romans had amassed over 1 500 years of conquest and expansion. The barbarians had laid their swords against one another, defeating army upon army, until the mightiest among them were ready to march and plunder their way to the ultimate prize: the ramparts of Rome – even taller and more formidable than the walls you will find, crowned with razor wire, in the genteel suburbs of Johannesburg. The fortifications that encircled that ancient citadel were thought to be unassailable.

But one morning, Valentinian, the emperor, was shaken awake by his servant, who said, 'Emperor, the barbarians are at the gates!' At their helm, as it turned out, was a military commander, an emperor himself, who was so fearsome, so ruthless, that he had become known far and wide by a battle name that was chilling in its portent: Flagellum Dei, or the Scourge of God. Today we know this warrior better as Attila the Hun. In Rome, the emperor, sleepy-eyed, stood on the balcony of his villa, with its commanding panorama of the seven hills of his beloved city, and what he saw was something even more frightening than the massed armies, the rabble of babblers, the barbarians at the gates. What he saw was the future, raging on his doorstep.

The world turns as we sleep, and in the quiet hours comes the revolution. The empires of our dreams crumble into dust, and in their stirrings, strange and curious new worlds arise. To begin with, we blame the barbarians – where did they come from so suddenly, and why did nobody warn us?

But the real onslaught has its origins in a far more powerful and sweeping force: the whirlwind of change.

Look at the amalgam of plastic and glass and rare earth metals that you hold in your hand. A glossy slab of connectivity, convenience and access to knowledge and information that we have all come to take for granted. But a smartphone is more, much more, than the sum of its parts. A smartphone is a slayer of empires. It slays the empire of physical books; of print newspapers; of hardbound encyclopaedias; of dedicated point-and-shoot cameras; of video cameras; of folding road maps; of portable GPS devices; of gaming devices; of hand-held voice recorders; of paper dictionaries; of portable calculators; of alarm clocks; of photo albums; of music players; of pocket diaries; of broadcast television; of landline telephones. And even of smartphones themselves: remember the once mighty, once unassailable behemoth of cellular devices, the BB? If you have momentarily forgotten what BB stands for, you're not alone. The BlackBerry was once the flagship of a global business worth almost $20 billion in annual revenue, shipping 7 million phones a year, and with 85 million subscribers worldwide. The phones were as beloved by business executives, because of their rock-solid security, as they were by teenagers, because of their thumb-friendly keyboards and instant messaging service. In its heyday, 'BB me' was as ubiquitous an injunction as 'WhatsApp me' is today. But then something happened. A barbarian pitched up at the gate.

It was a sleek black slab, mysteriously devoid of buttons on its façade, in defiance of all logic and the proven market preference for the tactile user interface. It looked like an alien artefact, a pocket-sized version of the towering obelisk from *2001: A Space Odyssey*. But this was 2007, and the artefact in question was the first Apple iPhone. What was BlackBerry's reaction to this stranger, this outsider, this non-belonger in their midst? It was twofold, according to *Losing the Signal*, a book on the company's spectacular rise and fall, by Jacquie McNish and Sean Silcoff. The first reaction was a stunned bepuzzlement. 'How did they do that?' wondered Mike Lazaridis, founder and vice chairman of BlackBerry, in reference to the iPhone's wide range of features and notable absence of a detachable battery. After the device had been disassembled in the lab, revealing the secret of its superpower – the entire phone was in effect a battery, with a small logic board attached to it – came the second reaction, which was a smug shrug, an imperious 'mxm' at Apple's impertinence in taking on the market leader.

'We'll be fine,' said BlackBerry's co-CEO, Jim Balsillie. Which was probably pretty much the same thing the last emperor of Rome said when he stood on his balcony and saw Attila the Hun camped out at the gate.

In 2009, at the peak of its fortunes, BlackBerry commanded almost 25 per cent of the global smartphone market. By the fourth quarter of 2016, its share had fallen to 0.048 per cent, which is a more polite way of saying zero. What went wrong? Let's look for the answer by focusing on a counter-example of what went right, for a company that also heard the warning of the barbarians at the gate – and then went out and changed the locks.

In 1998, an American software entrepreneur named Reed Hastings launched a company that in time would grow to become one of the most successful logistics and distribution enterprises in the world. He called it Netflix. On the face of it, it was a movie rental company, a mail-order version of Blockbuster (remember Blockbuster? Remember video stores?), supplying DVDs by first-class post to its customers on a subscription basis. The main attraction, aside from the catalogue of more than 50 000 movies, was that there were no late fees or shipping charges. For your $17,99 a month, you could order a constant stream of three titles at a time, with no monthly limits, and when you were done watching, you would pop the DVDs in the mail and wait for the next batch to arrive. You hardly had to get up from your couch.

But the engine of the operation was not the 'flix' in Netflix. The engine was the 'net': a sophisticated network of countrywide shipping centres, backed by software to manage the complex process of receiving, sorting and dispatching an inventory of more than 40 million DVD titles. How could your neighbourhood brick-and-mortar Blockbuster hope to compete with a logistics and distribution operation on that scale? By 2005, Netflix already had more than 4,5 million subscribers on its books, and Blockbuster was well on its way to going bust. Within five years, the once unassailable giant of home entertainment would file for bankruptcy, a fate that could have been avoided had Blockbuster taken up an earlier offer to go into partnership with Netflix. But the CEO at the time, John Antioco, turned the mail-order upstart down, on the grounds that Netflix was 'a very small niche business'. In the annals of short-sighted business decisions, that's right up there with Decca Records rejecting the Beatles in 1962, on the grounds that guitar bands were 'on their way out'.

But the truth is, Netflix could just as easily have gone out of business, had it not heeded the sound of thundering hooves and the battle cries of the barbarians gathering at the gate. What could be more convenient, for a lover of home movies, than to choose your movies on the internet and have them shipped to you by post? The answer, of course, lay in a science-fiction dream that became reality with the rise of fast and affordable broadband, making it possible to transmit your movies in the form of bits and bytes, straight from a server to your own personal computer. A couch potato's heaven.

In 2007, Netflix introduced the practice known as streaming, and today that stream has become an ocean, with more than 105 million subscribers in 190 countries getting their movies and TV series direct from the source. What kind of business is Netflix in today? It's no longer logistics and distribution. It's data and analytics. The real secret of Netflix is the way it uses the net to build an uncannily accurate, minutely personalised profile of each of its customers, based on the flix they've watched and the flix they're likely to like. These monetisable insights have allowed Netflix to become so powerful as a tastemaker that the company has moved beyond streaming other people's movies, and into the production of its own content, putting it in the same big-player league as Disney and Time Warner.

What Netflix has done right – looking over its shoulder, gearing up for the future, building systems that can withstand the disruption and destruction of its business models – is exactly what BlackBerry did wrong. 'We'll be fine' isn't a mantra for survival. It's a self-fulfilling prophecy of doom. To stay the way you are in a world that keeps changing the way it is, is to invite the future to leave you behind.

Every now and again, as part of my venture capital programme, I meet a young start-up hopeful who needs funding to put a good business idea into practice. And I'll ask, 'So, what do you do for a living?' And he'll say, 'I have a job.'

'Why don't you leave your job and start the business?' To which he'll say: 'I can't, because I need the income.'

That is not the way entrepreneurs think. The entrepreneur thinks: this is never going to happen if I don't get out there and make it happen. They can repossess my car if they want. I'll figure all that out later.

But let me dwell for a moment here on the difference between change and transformation. Change is how the tadpole becomes the frog. It starts as a blip, a black dot, an embryo encased in jelly. Then it spawns, a little flicker of a creature with a head and a tail and a pair of feathery gills. It develops a layer of skin that covers the gills. It sprouts back legs, and then front legs, allowing it to climb and manoeuvre around its watery environment. Soon, the tail disappears. The tadpole becomes the frog. It hops out of the water and announces its arrival with a croak. That is change.

Now consider the caterpillar. It starts as a hatchling, emerging from the egg as a patterned, many-legged organism whose primary purpose in life is to eat. It eats and eats, sheds its skin over and over, and then, one day, attaches itself to a twig or a leaf, building for itself a chrysalis in which, once again, it eats. But this time, hard as this may be to digest, it eats itself. It dissolves into a soup of enzymes, in which groups of cells begin organising and mutating into shapes – eyes, legs, wings. The chrysalis opens. A new creature emerges. Technically, it is known as an imago, the final, fully developed stage in the metamorphosis of an insect. It rests its wings for a while, acquainting itself with the state of the world. The tremor of the air, the force of the sun. It stirs, it flutters, and it lifts off into the sky. The butterfly has been born. That is transformation.

In the modern age, it is not enough merely to change. One must transform. But it's hard. And harder still for those of us who must weave the chrysalis with the weight of history hemming us in.

Let's go back to that young wannabe entrepreneur, whose ambition is constrained by his natural need to earn a steady income. Let's say he takes the wild and crazy leap of faith, and gets the funding to pursue his dreams. Let's say he stays in a far-flung township on the East Rand of Johannesburg, somewhere like, well, Wattville. Now, apartheid, as we know, wasn't a system only of racial discrimination. It was a system of spatial discrimination, and that system lingers in the spaces millions of people still occupy, on the fringes of cities, far from the suburbs with their neatly ordered office parks. Let's say our aspirant entrepreneur has to get from Wattville to Woodmead, a distance of over 40 kilometres, to get started at the enterprise development agency that is funding his dream. In the darkest hour before dawn, he hops on board a taxi, then takes a train, walks five kilometres or so to the office park, arrives tired, sweaty and hungry, gets told that he doesn't look the part and needs to up his game, and gets given an 80-page business plan, 20 pages of which contain financial projections.

Yes, he has a passing grade in maths matric, but because the passing grade is only 33 per cent, the projections are way above his ability, and he messes them up, gets into a panic, doesn't sleep, messes them up again, and gets to work two hours late in the morning because of a taxi strike. Will he ever be able to make it as an entrepreneur? Will he ever be able to transform? Will his dreams ever take wing and fly?

Funding entrepreneurship in South Africa isn't the problem. There is plenty of venture capital to go round. The problem is finding people who are worthy of the funding, and the problem inside that problem is a structural one: we need to go where the entrepreneurs are, not where we are.

The barbarians knocking at our gate are the ghosts of the past. They haunt us and hold us back. We will only be able to overcome them if we shift from our safe and comfortable spaces, if we go out into the world beyond the walls, to unlearn what we know and learn what we don't yet understand.

Sometimes, when we venture from our moorings, it can be good to leave our baggage behind, and wait for it to catch up with us on the next flight from home. Until then, all we need to get things moving is a simple acknowledgement that the future can and must be better than today. Mxm!

10

A Letter to Africa

Dear Africa,

You are the mother who gave birth to me. You heard my first cry, you nursed me, nurtured me, sang me to sleep, on the whisper of the wind and the lull of the ocean on the shore. You coaxed me from crawling into walking, you picked me up when I fell, you soothed me, comforted me, wiped away my tears. You taught me my name, but it was your name I spoke, when I learnt that you would hear me and answer my call, just as, Africa, you call to me too. I hear your voice in the rustle of the grass, the chorus of the birds, the quickening of my pulse in the quietness of the night. I hear you in the rumour of thunder on the horizon, in the roar of a river in flood.

    I hear you in the rush of the traffic on the freeway, drawn towards the glint of the dawn on the towers of steel and glass. I hear you in the rhythm of the machines on the factory floor, the spark of fire on metal that forges the engine of industry in motion. I hear you in the stirring of my blood, which surges with the blood of those who travelled before me, the warriors who charged into battle on the tide of the rolling hills.

I hear you in the dust that rises to cloud the face of the sun, in the songs of celebration and lament that echo to the edges of heaven. I hear you, Africa, in the voice of my father. You held me in your arms and looked into my eyes, to see the reflection of the hope that I would one day lead the better, easier life that you had been denied. You took me by the hand, you led me, guided me, shared with me the stories of the struggle that would one day set me free. You taught me to be unafraid of the world that lay outside me, and of the power that lay within.

You taught me that I could be the equal of any other, in my quest to be greater. You taught me that I had a voice, and that I should use it to make myself heard. You showed me that courage is the pathway to survival, and that kindness is the road to respect. Africa, you are the teacher who opened my eyes. You planted in me the seed of curiosity, you quenched my thirst to learn who I was, where I had come from, who

I could strive to be. You pointed me to the place of our genesis, the point on the map where humanity was born, where the first of our species rose to look at the stars, to wonder what lay beyond them, to set off in search of the answers.

You are the footprints that were washed away by the waves, where the hunter-gatherers walked alone for hundreds of years, before the tall ships came. You are the shadow of the gods who shifted shape to become the wild animals of the wide-open plains. You are the ghost of the slaves who were wrenched from their homes, to be shipped in chains across the stormy seas. You are the spirit of the chieftains, the kings, the builders of empires and city states that crumbled into ruin and sank beneath the desert sands.

You are the lost, the abandoned, the displaced, whose histories have been forgotten, whose legends have never been retold. You are the souls in restless exile, the wanderers, the removed, forever dispossessed of the land on which their forefathers were born. You are the heroes who stood up, who fought back, who shed their blood and gave their lives, so that those who followed in their footsteps could be free. Africa, you are my grandmother, who walked with back bent from years of selfless toil, and yet who stood proud and tall in the glow of her grandchildren's achievements.

You are the scientist, the doctor, the entrepreneur, the artist, the poet, the engineer, the farmer, the lawyer, the teacher, the dancer, the nurse. You are the student who stands on the stage and raises her fist as the sash straddles her shoulders, the first in her family to graduate, the first to walk out into the world and make her dreams come true. Africa, you are my children, who are too small, too innocent, to know of a time when the horizons of their possible tomorrows would have been defined and confined by the colour of their skin.

You are the hope that rises, the strength that conquers, the pride that defies. You are 54 nations, you are 1 500 languages, you are 1.2 billion people, from Cape Agulhas in the south to Ras ben Sakka in the north, from Pointe des Almadies in the west to Ras Hafun in the east. You are all of us who were born here, all of us who wandered here, all of us who choose to make this our home. You are the past that shaped us, the present that sustains us, the future that dares, challenges and inspires us. Africa, you are me, and I am proud to be,

Your son,
Vusi Thembekwayo

About the Author

VUSI THEMBEKWAYO is the founder and CEO of MyGrowthFund and IC Knowledge Bureau. He is a venture capitalist, a sought-after global business speaker and the author of *The Magna Carta of Exponentiality* – a change agent who has helped to build and transform businesses in South Africa and abroad.

He does more than inspire a revolution, he initiates it. He has been a catalyst for change in businesses across the globe through expertise in strategy, leadership and organisational culture. Through his international speaking engagements, more than 21 countries and 350 000 audiences have experienced Vusi.

Set in 11.5 on 18pt Ehrhardt
Cover by Fuel Design
Book design by Nazli Jacobs
Edited by Mark Ronan
Proofread by Lisa Compton
Commissioning editor: Gill Moodie

Printed by **novus print**, a Novus Holdings company